Interpersonal Communication

How do people communicate with each other in their face-to-face meetings and conversations? Do we really understand all the interpersonal codes and signals which we use and react to? *Interpersonal Communication* provides a comprehensive introduction for students of the how and why of interpersonal communication. Peter Hartley uses research and theory from Social Psychology, Sociology, and Linguistics to provide a framework for understanding how we use language, gestures and facial expressions to communicate.

The book is divided into three parts. Part one outlines the main concepts necessary to understand both the skills and the process of interpersonal communication; part two looks at these processes in more detail and discusses their everyday applications and implications. For example, what evidence is there to support the claim that our gestures and facial expressions reveal to others what we 'really' mean? Can we trust our first impressions of people, or should we be more cautious? Part three examines situations – for example, interaction between groups of people – where 'more than interpersonal' communication is involved.

Interpersonal Communication will be an invaluable resource for students and teachers of A-level and undergraduate courses in Communication Studies and Social Sciences, and also to anyone who would like to know more about how we communicate.

Peter Hartley is Head of Academic Development in the School of Cultural Studies, Sheffield Hallam University.

Interpersonal Communication

Peter Hartley

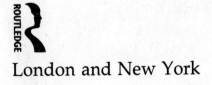

London and New York

First published 1993
by Routledge
11 New Fetter Lane, London EC4P 4EE

Simultaneously published in the USA and Canada
by Routledge
29 West 35th Street, New York, NY 10001

Printed in Great Britain by
T.J. Press (Padstow) Ltd, Padstow, Cornwall

British Library Cataloguing in Publication Data
Hartley, Peter
  Interpersonal Communication
  I. Title
  302.2

Library of Congress Cataloging in Publication Data
Hartley, Peter
  Interpersonal communication / Peter Hartley.
    p.   cm.
  Includes bibliographical references and index.
  1. Interpersonal communication. I. Title.
  BF637.C45H35   1993
  153.6—dc20
  92–29380
ISBN 0–415–01384–4
      0–415–01385–2 (pbk)

Contents

Acknowledgements

Thanks are due to many people who helped in developing this book. Needless to say I am responsible for any flaws in the final version.

Special thanks go to:

- Guy Fielding, who collaborated on the initial outline

- Andrew Beck, Gary Radford, and Jane Weston, who commented on various drafts

- Julia, James and David, who provided various combinations of inspiration and practical help

- Jane Armstrong and Rebecca Barden, for their patience and encouragement well beyond the call of duty

Foreword

Introductions to textbooks can range from a brief paragraph to mini-novels which tell you almost everything which is in the rest of the book. Avoiding these extremes, I have simply tried to answer a few questions which may help you decide whether you actually want to read any further.

What are the aims of this book?

The main aim is to provide a basic introductory text on interpersonal communication, ie face-to-face communication between two people. So I have tried to:

- explain the special or distinctive characteristics of interpersonal communication
- identify the component parts of interpersonal communication
- explain how these components relate to one another
- explain the most important features of the skills involved in communicating with other people
- contrast the characteristics of interpersonal communication with other forms of communication

Although the main concepts and theories are drawn from research in the social sciences, I have tried to avoid social science jargon unless it really helps to express the arguments. My aim was to make this text readable and interesting.

How is the book organised?

The major sections

In section A, I try to establish a coherent framework for understanding interpersonal communication. As well as offering a definition and model of the process, I discuss the major skills involved and show how these different approaches to the subject are related.

Section B provides a more detailed analysis of the major components of interpersonal communication.

Section C introduces situations which involve other people but where there are processes over and above the ones outlined in section B. For example, communication in groups is not the same as communicating with one other person - there are different influences at work.

Within chapters

Each chapter is sub-divided into major sections which are listed at the beginning of each chapter. Each major section focusses on one important question or issue.

At the end of each chapter, there is a list of notes which includes:

- details of references cited in the text
- further comments for anyone wishing to explore the topic in more detail
- references and suggestions for further reading.

What is the best way to read this book?

This may seem a nonsensical question. Surely you simply read any book from beginning to end. I disagree. That may be the way to read a novel on a train journey but is not the way we read many books. This text will be read by different people for different purposes and so you may wish to choose a different approach. For example:

If you are reading this simply from general interest in the topic, then I suggest that you

- read Chapters 1 and 2 fairly quickly
- concentrate on the aspects that interest you in the remaining chapters

- ignore the notes unless anything strikes you as particularly interesting

If you are reading this as a student on a course, then I suggest that you

- read Section A first
- read subsequent chapters in the order in which they crop up in your course
- when you read a chapter you skim-read it first before going through it more slowly and checking the notes

Whatever your approach, I hope you find this book helpful and interesting. And that you find some ideas which you can use to make your own communication more satisfying and effective.

Language and sexism

In my own teaching, I warn students to avoid sexist language and expressions. So I have tried to practise what I preach. In this book, "he" is always male and "she" is always female, except in a few of the direct quotes from other authors who have obviously not read Miller and Swift. [1]

Peter Hartley
October 1992

Notes

1   Anyone who is not convinced that sexist language should be avoided both for the sake of accuracy and fairness is referred to this excellent book:

C. Miller and K. Swift (1989) *The Handbook of Non-Sexist Writing*, 2nd edn, The Women's Press

Section A

Deciding what we mean by interpersonal communication

1

Defining interpersonal communication

In this chapter, I shall:

- introduce the definition of interpersonal communication which is used throughout this book

- outline a number of propositions about interpersonal communication which can be developed from this definition and which have important practical and theoretical implications

1

How can we define interpersonal communication?

Most books which can be used as textbooks start with a chapter which tries to define the subject matter and approach. This is an obvious place to start if you are completely new to the subject. But what about a text on communication? Surely we all know what communication is? Isn't it a major part of all our daily lives?

One writer has gone so far as to say that:[1]

> all social interaction is necessarily communicative and any social process presumes a communication process

In other words, anything we do with other people must involve communication.

If communication is so "universal", then perhaps I can assume that everyone knows what it is, and move straight on to the next chapter! Unfortunately, things are not so straightforward. If you read a number of textbooks on communication, you will find a variety of definitions which emphasise different things. You will also find considerable practical differences in everyday life. Some people seem to regard the essence of communication as "being able to speak and write proper English" whereas others would argue that "good communicators are good listeners". So it is important to clarify what I am talking about.

To return to the academic debate, I can easily produce a list of fifteen general definitions of communication which represent rather different ideas or emphases![2] A similar variety of definitions also exists for interpersonal communication. As well as verbal definitions, there are many models of interpersonal communication, often expressed as diagrams involving numerous boxes and arrows.[3] In this book, I have attempted to synthesise as many of these ideas as possible to highlight the fundamental processes.

I can best introduce my approach by comparing events which obviously involve people communicating with one another in different contexts:

(a) Two friends discussing their recent holidays over a cup of coffee

(b) An argument between a married couple concerning the behaviour of their teenage son

(c) A seminar discussion between a lecturer and four of her students

(d) A telephone call to a local store to enquire about the availability of a particular product

(e) A letter from a daughter to her parents about her experiences of working abroad

(f) A trader touting his "never to be repeated" bargains in a street market

(g) Martin Luther King addressing 100,000 demonstrators at the Washington Memorial in 1968

(h) The Queen's Christmas Day broadcast

(i) Sitting in a cinema watching a film

(j) Sitting at home watching the news on TV

(k) Reading a daily newspaper

All these examples involve communication and they involve people. But they are very different experiences because of the different processes involved. For example, they can be grouped in terms of major differences:

The nature of the audience
Items f-k all involve large audiences ranging from the crowd in the market (f) to potentially the whole society (h or k). Thus, the receivers of the communication are not known as individuals to the sender. In some cases the sender is an individual but in others the sender is a group or organisa-

tion, or an individual acting on behalf of an organisation (eg the newsreader in j).

Relationship

Items a-e, in contrast, all involve events where the participants are specific individuals who are known to one another. This knowledge of the other person is a very important aspect of the interaction.

Medium of communication

Items a-c are purely face-to-face whereas items d, e and g-k use some medium of communication in between the senders and receivers. Item f may use some form of medium, eg a public address system, but this will depend on the size of audience and the strength of the trader's lungs!

Interpersonal

Only examples a, b and c in the above list are examples of what this book defines as interpersonal comunication, i.e. they have the following characteristics:

- communication from one individual to another
- communication which is face-to-face
- both the form and content of the communication reflect the personal characteristics of the individuals as well as their social roles and relationships

Table 1 summarises the different forms of communication which I have mentioned. It does not cover some forms of communication which I shall discuss later in the book - within and between groups.

Table 1: different forms of communication

	Individual to individual	Individual to mass audience	Group to mass audience
Face-to-face communication	1	2	3
Technologically mediated communication	4	5	6

Only box 1 fully satisfies the definition of interpersonal communication used in this book. All the other boxes are situations which involve other factors.

What does this definition involve?

Any textbook definition will have a number of practical and theoretical implications. The most important implications which can be developed from this definition of interpersonal communication are contained in the following seven propositions:

1 Face-to-face meetings

Interpersonal communication involves face-to-face meetings between two participants

I deliberately exclude any communication which I would call "mediated", such as a telephone conversation, where some artificial medium carries the conversation between the participants.

This is because every medium has particular characteristics which can have implications for communication. In everyday life, we may not be aware of these characteristics or may never consider them. This lack of awareness can lead to misunderstandings. This issue is discussed more fully in Chapter 10.

This proposition also excludes situations where one person is addressing an audience for some reason, eg giving a lecture, an after-dinner speech. Again this calls for some special principles which are not covered in this book.

2 Roles

Interpersonal communication involves two people in varying roles and relationships to one another

I discuss the concept of role in much more detail in Chapter 6 but for the moment I am using the concept to cover both formal positions such as policeman, teacher etc, and the more informal roles which we may take on in some situations, eg the person who always intervenes to try to alleviate conflict in a group of friends - the "harmoniser".

This emphasis on roles and relationships may seem blindingly obvious but some writers do talk of interpersonal communication in a rather more specialised sense. For example, consider the following quote from John Stewart:[4]

> Interpersonal communication happens between PERSONS, not between roles or masks or stereotypes.
> Interpersonal communication can happen between you and me only when each of us recognizes and shares some of what makes us human beings AND is aware of some of what makes the other person too.

Stewart, in common with many American authors, is concerned that people *should* communicate with one another in a particular way. He advocates that we should communicate in order to develop personal relationships of the following sort:

- where there is a high degree of trust

- where each person is prepared to discuss openly their feelings and personal history (often referred to as self-disclosure, which I discuss in Chapter 3)

- where there is genuine and mutual liking or caring between the participants

Thus, Stewart also talks about "non-interpersonal" communication where people simply communicate "what they have to".

An example may make this clearer. Have you ever been in a situation where someone whom you do not know well but who is in a position of authority over you (such as a temporary teacher) has asked "how are you?". You may have been feeling down but answered "fine" or "OK". Without thinking about it, you recognised that the original question was simply a social gesture - it was not a "genuine" enquiry about your well-being. The person was asking because they felt obliged to do so rather than because they really cared about you. So you replied with a polite but dishonest reply - to use Stewart's definition, you communicated "non-interpersonally". What would have happened if you had blurted out all your woes and tribulations - would the other person have been able, or willing, to cope?

This book leaves the ethical questions of how we should, or should not, communicate to you to discuss and decide for yourself - it adopts a broader and more "neutral" definition of interpersonal communication and follows a more descriptive approach.

3 Two-way

Interpersonal communication is ALWAYS two-way

The so-called linear model of communication[5] is one of the most popular ways of representing communication in a diagram. This model suggests that our communication is linear and one-way. In other words, it consists of messages flowing from sender to receiver along particular channels,

7

although there may be some interference (noise) along the way.

This model is usually expressed in a diagram as follows:

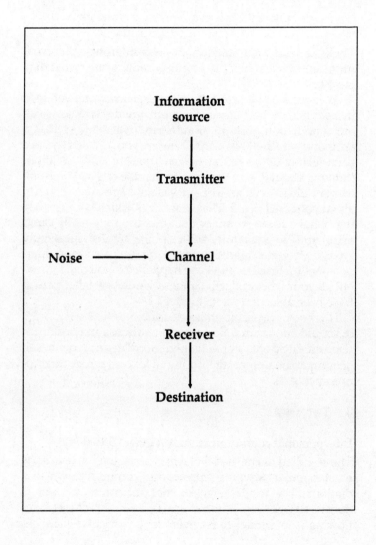

**Information
source**

↓

Transmitter

↓

Noise ——→ **Channel**

↓

Receiver

↓

Destination

Unfortunately this model neglects one of the fundamental points in this book - in interpersonal situations there is *always* a two-way flow of communication. For example, imagine a conversation where A is telling B about the good time he had on holiday. A does most if not all of the talking. Does that make him *the* sender? He is also able to observe B's reactions to what he is saying - receiving information from the way B is acting as an audience. In this sense B is also both receiver and sender. He may grunt, nod, look attentive - all MAY be acts of communication which are interpreted by the other person. It is no accident that one of the social skills which psychologists have recently focussed attention on is listening, one aspect of which is giving feedback to the other person. You can train people to become better listeners and this is a very important social skill (See Chapter 3).

4 Meaning

Interpersonal communication does not simply involve the exchange of messages. It essentially involves the creation and exchange of meaning

One important implication of the linear model of communication follows from its concern with "the message" . This implies that we can arrive at an accurate and unambiguous statement of whatever was communicated. And it also suggests that we shall be able to verify that statement by checking with the participants as well as any observers present. In fact, this is extremely difficult if not impossible to achieve. Whereas we might not agree that "all human behaviour is ambiguous",[6] just about anything anyone says *could* be interpreted in a number of ways.

Luckily this does not happen all of the time or we would live in a completely chaotic world. For example, how would you interpret the following question from neighbour A:

"Did you have a good time last night?"

This could be a casual, friendly gesture. But what could it mean?

- Is A behaving genuinely? Perhaps he is being cynical and deliberately trying to "soften you up" so that he can come and borrow something off you?

- On the other hand, is it a subtle accusation of rowdy behaviour? Is it a warning for next time you have a party?

- Is it a deliberate play on the fact that A was not invited, designed to make you feel uncomfortable?

- Is it a more dejected expression of A's loneliness?

All of these are *possible* interpretations of A's message. Some of these may seem very unlikely but this depends on the meaning which you and A attach to your encounter. And this will depend on a *number* of factors discussed later in this book, such as the state of the relationship between you and A, or any of your perceptual biasses which might influence your reactions to A.

So this analysis suggests that we must look very carefully at the meaning which people attach to particular events before we can really understand the communication which is taking place.

On the other hand, we can learn a great deal about communication without delving very deeply into personal beliefs and interpretations. For example, there have been a number of studies recently which have examined how teachers in schools communicate to their pupils, often using some method of classifying the messages that teachers send, eg do they ask questions, encourage pupils etc. Thus the messages are classified in terms of their "obvious" meaning. There is no attempt to study in detail the possible interpretations that pupils place on their teacher's behaviour. Nonetheless useful and interesting results emerge. One fairly typical finding, which comes as rather a shock to teachers, is that they do not always do what they think they do. For example, teachers who claim to be equally "fair" to boys and girls may still be directing their attention towards the boys when they expect boys will do better in that subject.[7]

The issue I have just raised is one aspect of a very deep-rooted argument within social science, ie whether people are mainly *passive* responders to external stimuli or whether they adopt a more *active* approach in interpreting and making sense of the world. I favour the latter position which suggests that when we try to understand communication fully we must be aware of the meaning which people attach to events and surroundings.

Thus, in order to fully understand communication, we need to look at how individuals make sense of the situation they are in.

But does this mean that we cannot generalise from situation to situation? If we accept that everyone is unique then does this mean that everyone will interpret events differently? And does this then mean that all communication can only be understood with reference to the specific individuals involved? Is all communication totally personal?

I cannot go along with this line of argument. There must be *some* shared meaning for there to be any communication at all! If we all lived in *completely* unique and idiosyncratic "perceptual worlds" we could not talk to one another. There would be no basis for any language system to work. It may be difficult for you to understand how I interpret particular events (and vice versa) but I could explain my interpretation to you, given sufficient time and patience.

5 Intention

Interpersonal communication is partly or wholly intentional

All would agree, for example, that a measly face can be INFORMATIVE to a qualified onlooker. But is it useful to speak of the sufferer himself (who may be unaware of it) as COMMUNICATING this information? Is there no distinction to be made between the passive manifestation of a symptom and the deliberate (even if instinctive) production of words or non-verbal behaviour (including perhaps pointing to the spots) CALCULATED to inform the observer? [8]

It is not very useful to think of someone "communicating" that they have measles because their face is lumpy or spotty, and this book concentrates on situations where participants do have purposes or intentions which they *wish* to communicate. On the other hand it is often very difficult in practice to draw a precise distinction between informative and communicative behaviour.

6 Process

Interpersonal communication is an ongoing process rather than an event or series of events
When you think of an event you usually think of something very definite which happens, and which has a definite start and a definite finish. It can be misleading to think of interpersonal communication in this way.

There are a number of more academic arguments which emphasise the importance of understanding interpersonal communication as a continuous unfolding process[9] but for the moment I shall take a practical example - a selection interview.

Imagine you are a candidate, sitting in the waiting room. At what point do you start to communicate with your interviewers - when you arrive in the reception area? when you answer the first question? when you walk into the interview room? when you stand up to greet the member of the selection panel who has come out to collect you? Your behaviour at *all* these points could have an important bearing on what happens because of the ongoing process of communication. There is also the complication that you have already communicated to the interviewers through your application form - what stereotypes and preconceptions are already there in their minds? There may also be more subtle social influences - at least one boss I have known took very serious notice of how his secretary showed prospective job-hunters into his room. The way she introduced the candidate always included very subtle opinions on his or her "suitability".

7 Time

Interpersonal communication is cumulative over time

You cannot erase a remembered pain.[10]

Whatever a person says to you today will be interpreted on the basis of what they have said to you in the past and also what you expect them to say. If you are trying to understand communication between people who have communicated before, then you need to take into account the history of their relationship as this might well affect how they interpret each other's remarks at the moment.

Conclusion

This chapter should have clarified what this book is about. Hopefully it should also have convinced you that interpersonal communication is not as simple or straightforward as many people seem to believe. Although this may have seemed a fairly theoretical chapter, the issues raised have important practical implications. For example, we often act *as if* communication was linear - as if there *was* a clear and unambiguous definition of the message and that feedback was unimportant. We do so at our peril, as will be demonstrated in the following chapters.

Notes

1   This quote is taken from an introductory text written by a sociologist. You may like to compare our different approaches. He does provide a very interesting chapter on theories and models which you may like to read after you have read Chapters 1 and 2 of this book.

D. McQuail (1975) *Communication*, 1st edn, Longman

2   The list can be found in the article by Dance who goes on to discuss major differences between the definitions. The article is also published in the collection by Porter and Roberts.

F. E. X. Dance (1970) "The Concept of Communication", *Journal of Communication*, vol 20, pp 201-210

L. W. Porter and K. H. Roberts (1977) *Communication in Organisations*, Penguin

3   You may like to contrast John Fiske's discussion with other versions, eg the chapter in McQuail (see note 1).

J. Fiske (1982) *Introduction to Communication Studies*, Methuen

4   For a typical example of this approach, see :

J. Stewart and G. D'Angelo (1975) *Together: Communicating Interpersonally*, Addison-Wesley

5   The model is based upon the very influential early work of Shannon and Weaver which is discussed (and often misquoted!) in virtually every textbook of communication. A very clear introduction to their approach and its more sophisticated development is contained in the article by Klaus Krippendorff. Also see the book by John Fiske (Note 3 above).

Many "popular" books on communication also adopt what is effectively a linear model. For a recent example, see Chapter 1 of the book by Malcolm Peel.

K. Krippendorff (1975) "Information Theory",
in G. J. Hanneman and W. J. McEwen, eds,
Communication and Behaviour, Addison Wesley

M. Peel (1990) *Improving Your Communication Skills*,
Kogan Page

6   This quote is associated with Abraham Maslow, a
very influential American psychologist who was
concerned that psychologists should pay more attention to promoting the positive or healthy side of
human beings. He believed that most of psychology
concentrated on human weaknesses or limitations and
did not provide useful information to help people
develop their abilities or potential. His theory of
human motivation suggests that humans have a
progressive series of needs culminating in the need to
realise their potential. This has proved very popular
and influential although it only has limited
supporting evidence. See Huczynski and Buchanan
(p 59ff) for a recent summary.

A. H. Maslow (1971) *The Farther Reaches of Human
Nature*, Viking Press

A. A. Huczynski and D. A. Buchanan (1991)
Organizational Behaviour, 2nd edn, Prentice Hall

7   This is a specific example of a situation where someone behaves in accordance with their expectations
even though they may not be consciously aware of
them. This issue is discussed again in Chapter 5.

8   McKay provides a very detailed discussion of this
issue in an article which is fairly complex - definitely
not for beginners. The article is in a book by Robert
Hinde which contains a number of interesting
approaches.

R. A. Hinde, ed, (1972) *Nonverbal Communication*,
Cambridge University Press

9 This argument is very strongly argued by Danziger in an important book which I refer to on several occasions:

K. Danziger (1976) *Interpersonal Communication*, Pergamon

10 I first heard this remark in a talk by Fred Herzberg, the well-known American management consultant. He was reminding managers that employees have good memories - if you treat them badly they will never forget it!

2

The process of interpersonal communication

In this chapter I shall:

- discuss how we can best understand interpersonal communication
- outline a model of interpersonal communication, using examples to illustrate the components

How can we understand interpersonal communication?

Social scientists interested in interpersonal communication have usually adopted one of the following approaches:

- developing a model of interpersonal communication - trying to identify the components of the process

- identifying the behaviours which are associated with effective interpersonal communication - defining the skills of interpersonal communication

In practice these approaches are inevitably interlinked. For example, you cannot really identify skills without a good understanding of the process. I shall say more on this later.

In this chapter I shall concentrate on the first of these approaches. I shall briefly discuss what this involves and then explain my model of interpersonal communication.

In the next chapter, I shall discuss what it means to explain interpersonal communication as skilled behaviour and give a few examples to illustrate the value of such an approach. I shall also explain how the two approaches depend upon one another. To fully understand interpersonal communication you need to integrate both approaches.

What does understanding interpersonal communication involve?

If you say you understand something then you should be able to answer specific questions about it. For example, suppose you say that you understand what a compact disc is - could you answer the folowing questions about it?:

- how were CDs first developed?

- how is a CD made?

- how do CD players work?

- what are the main differences between a CD and a vinyl album?
- how, when and where are CDs used?

You may be able to answer most if not all these questions. So there are degrees of understanding depending on how much you know. But there are also different types of understanding depending on your purposes. For example, you may feel you understand compact discs because you can use them correctly. This is rather different from understanding their electronics - such intricacies as digital-analog conversion and error correction. You may not want to explore these details because you really only want to listen to the music!

Applying this type of analysis to communication brings out similar points. Your understanding of interpersonal communication will depend on how much you know, based on what you have observed and the breadth of your experience. Your understanding will also depend upon your purposes and whether you want to inquire further. For example, later in the book there are some examples of sales' techniques. Sales representatives may be able to use interpersonal techniques very expertly without fully understanding how they really work. On the other hand, you may be able to "defeat" sales representatives if you understand their ploys.

The aim of this book is to provide understanding of how interpersonal communication "works" by exploring the "mechanics" of the process, looking at its various components and how they relate to one another. One way of doing this is by asking questions and you may have come across one classic definition of communication which uses a question approach:

Who says what
In which channel
To whom
With what effect

This definition[1] can be criticised - it does not take account of the different meanings which participants can perceive in the same situation. It also neglects the more subtle processes of communication - communication is not just talk! Finally it has limitations in that it does not take account of the social context in which the communication takes place.

These limitations could perhaps be overcome by adding additional questions. But then you could end up with a rather unwieldly list:

> When and where does communication occur?
> Who is involved?
> How do the people communicate?
> How does the communication develop over time?
> What roles are people adopting?
> How do they relate to one another?
> What is the physical setting?
> What do people say and do?
> What are they trying to achieve?
> How do people interpret each other's actions?

You can probably refine and add to this list. But a list of questions does not give a very clear idea of how the different factors are related to one another. So rather than pursue this approach further I shall develop a model of interpersonal communication which attempts to specify what is involved and how the components relate to one another.

What is a model?

A model is quite simply a scaled-down representation of some thing or event. You can identify the major characteristics of a good model by thinking about physical models. For example, if I built a model of a car out of old toilet roll tubes and then showed it to you, how would you judge it? You would probably ask a number of questions:

- does it look like a car?

- does it have all the important bits on it? eg are there four wheels, engine, exhaust etc.

- does it work? eg does the engine make the wheels go round? what happens if you turn the steering wheel?

- will Blue Peter like it?

The better the model, the more accurate and detailed it will be. But usually you have to reach some sort of compromise where you sacrifice some detail in order to make the model easy to build or operate.

These same considerations apply when you try to develop a theoretical model of something:

- the model should contain the major components

- it should show how these relate to one another

- it should be reasonably detailed

So I am aiming to provide a model for interpersonal communication which can satisfy these criteria.[2]

A model of interpersonal communication

My basic model of interpersonal communication is summarised in the diagram on the next page. The major boxes represent major components of the process.

Once you have read all this book and perhaps done further research, you may like to return to it and criticise it - does it live up to the following characteristics?:

- does the model highlight the most important characteristics of interpersonal communication?

- is it sufficiently detailed to be a useful basis for analysing everyday situations?

- does the model show how the different processes relate to one another?

As this is designed to be an introductory text, you should be able to pick some holes in the model once you have become more familiar with some of the relevant theories and research.

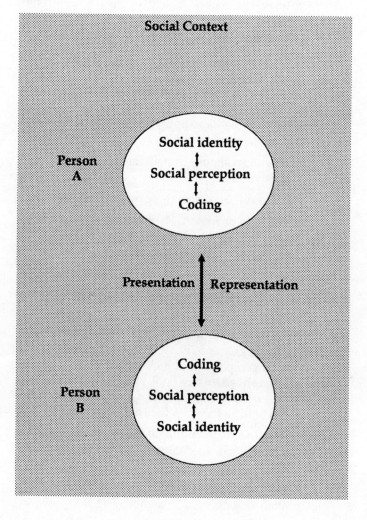

How does this model help?

Using the model to identify the components of the communication process should help us to understand what is going on in practical situations. So this section applies the components of the model to specific examples:

The case of Dr Poussaint

Consider the following real conversation between two people (A and B). If you want to test your understanding of communication you can think of your answers to the questions below before you turn the page and read my explanation.

The conversation

A.   "What's your name, boy?"

B.   "Dr Poussaint. I'm a physician."

A.   "What's your first name, boy?"

B.   "Alvin."

Questions

1.   Where and when did the conversation take place?

2.   What sort of people were A and B?

3.   After this conversation, B described his feelings:

"As my heart palpitated, I muttered in profound humiliation. . . For the moment, my manhood had been ripped from me. . . No amount of self-love could have salvaged my pride or preserved my integrity. . . (I felt) self-hate."

Why do you think he felt like this?

The situation

This conversation is a very vivid example of how someone can manipulate communication in order to serve their own, in this case, rather sadistic and racist ends. The conversation took place on a public street in the United States in 1967. A was a white police officer, Dr Poussaint was a black doctor.

Explanation

In order to understand this conversation you need to understand several factors which are identified in the model:

Social context
You need to understand the social context - how the time and the place influenced the actions and reactions. Dr Poussaint felt he had to answer the questions because of his social obligations and the power relations in a public place. A policeman may be "allowed" to ask personal questions in public without necessarily explaining why.

Social identities/perception
We also need to know how the two participants saw themselves (their social identity) and each other (social perception). Dr Poussaint saw himself as a respectable citizen and a professional person who normally received some degree of respect. He felt humiliated when this sense of identity was ignored. He saw the policeman as occupying a role of authority. As a result he had no choice but to act according to his obligations as a respectable law-abiding citizen.

Codes
The policeman had quite different intentions and you can deduce these from his use of codes which he must have been aware of.

I shall provide a more detailed definition of "codes" later on. For the moment, I shall talk about a code as a particular way of expressing a message which has a special meaning to a certain audience. I shall also leave aside the notions of presentation and representation which I shall explain later in this chapter.

As an example of the use of a special code, consider how the policeman first addressed Dr Poussaint. He used the term "boy" in a very deliberate way to make Dr Poussaint feel inferior. Obviously, he was not using the word in its literal meaning as he could see perfectly well that the doctor was a grown man. He probably also used visual codes to reinforce the cruel and dismissive message, eg not looking directly at Dr Poussaint while he was talking. You can see how "successful" he was in his aims when you read the interpretation which Dr Poussaint put upon his comments.

This conversation has been very thoroughly analysed by Susan Ervin-Tripp.[3] She concluded that the policeman deliberately used racial insults no less than three times in the course of the conversation, simply by breaking the rules of address which people normally obey in these situations.

A rule of address is a social rule which governs how you address the other person. For example do you call the other person "sir", or by their first name, or by their last name? These rules can be quite different in different societies. Social rules are discussed in more detail in Chapter 5 but as an example you can think of how you respond to different people in different situations in terms of the names you call them. And what names do they call you?

But to return to Dr Poussaint and the three insults:

- First of all, the policeman used the term "boy". He would never have used this expression if the doctor had been white.

- Secondly he ignored the perfectly reasonable answer he received from Dr Poussaint and asked for his first name without any justification.

- Thirdly he *repeated* the term "boy". He rubbed salt into the wounds quite viciously.

So while he showed a degree of "skill" in the use of communication to suit his purposes, that policeman blatantly demonstrated serious deficiencies as a human being.

The parking meter conversation

For another example to illustrate the model, try this short extract from a real conversation:[4]

A: "Dana succeeded in putting a penny in a parking meter today without being picked up."

B: "Did you take him to the record store?"

This conversation is very difficult to decipher unless you happen to know a number of things over and above the actual words spoken:

Social context
This conversation took place between two parents in their home just after the husband (A) had brought their son Dana home from nursery school.

Social identities
The couple see themselves as responsible parents who are interested in the welfare and development of their son.

Social perception
The couple see each other as caring and responsible parents. They regularily share information about the activities and progress of their son. Dana is now big enough to put a coin in a parking meter without help.

Codes
The term "picking up" is ambiguous unless you know that Dana is young and small. The husband is carrying a record and this prompts the question from his wife.

26

One important implication of this model is that the various components must be compatible for the communication to be effective. When I say "effective" I mean that the two parties take the same meaning from the interaction. Where this is not the case then misunderstanding or conflict is inevitable.

The final components

This leads me to the final two components of the model - presentation and representation. I have borrowed this distinction from Kurt Danziger.[5] He makes the important point that whenever we communicate we always do two things simultaneously:

Representation
We represent some information - we make some statement about the world around us.

Presentation
We present the information in a particular way, and this serves to define our relationship with the other person in a particular way.

An example which Danziger uses is the example of the salesman. Consider the following interchange between a salesman and Mrs Jones:

> "You like the special action brush then?"
> "Oh yes. "
> "And you understand how all these other features (points) will help you?"
> "Sure."
> "You said you appreciated the ease of operation particularly?"
> "That' s right."
> "So you're convinced that a Hoover will make your work easier?"
> "Hm hm."

"And you do admit that buying later won't help you
now, don't you?"
"I guess so."
"In fact you owe it to your family to get one now,
isn't that right?"
"Yeah. "
"So you have decided to take this model then?"
"O.K."

Danziger analyses not just *what* the salesman says (representation) but also *how* he says it (presentation). The salesman has a sequence of points which he makes. Each point is
skilfully phrased so that when she answers Mrs Jones is
compelled to present herself in a particular way. The salesman is laying a trap for Mrs Jones. Firstly, he recognises that
Mrs Jones will wish to be seen as caring, considerate and
reasonable. He starts by pointing out that Mrs Jones has seen
aspects of the product she likes and progressively builds
these up to become more significant. Mrs Jones is carried
along by the logic, and the speed and loaded phrasing of the
questions make it difficult for her to "reasonably" object.
Then the salesman brings in her "obligations" to her family
to clinch the deal. Having gradually committed herself to the
benefits of the product and not wishing to appear inconsist-
ent, she is unable to escape this final invitation.

We can also develop this analysis using the other components of my model. The salesman takes great care to present
himself as competent, trustworthy and friendly so that Mrs
Jones does not become suspicious (social perception). The
salesman makes very skilful use of language and nonverbal
behaviour (codes) to put pressure on Mrs Jones to act in line
with her feelings about herself as a responsible housewife
(social identity).

This example could be caricatured as an illustration of the
"gullible housewife" stereotype but it is far more fundamental than this. Men are just as susceptible to these techniques,
as I can testify from bitter personal experience at the hands
of double-glazing and vacuum-cleaner salesmen! Even if
you know what salesmen are trying to do you can still be

caught up in the emotions that they are trying to tap. However, knowing what is going on is the first step to resisting the pressure.

Mrs Jones could have dealt with the salesman rather differently if she had recognised how she was being manipulated and if she had been prepared to turn the tables on the salesman. She did not have to accept the social identity which the salesman was relying upon. For example, suppose she had been confronted by a salesman for a new line in children's food and suppose she adopted a somewhat different style of presentation and went on the attack (this example is also taken from Danziger):

> "You are interested in better nutrition and health for your family if it's possible to get it aren't you, Mrs Jones?"
> "No."
> "No?"
> "They're too healthy now. They're running me ragged. I'm going to start feeding them less. They've had too many vitamins, that's the trouble. They're going to burn themselves out."
> "But surely you want them to be properly fed?"
> "That's been the problem - too much food. I'm cutting them right off milk next week, soon's I use up the box of crystals. Maybe that'll help quieten my husband down nights."

The salesman's opening remark is based on the quite reasonable assumption that no respectable mother will deny that she is interested in her family's health. Once he has established this very small area of common ground and commitment then he can develop it further. If Mrs Jones refuses to present herself in this way then the salesman's pitch is completely undermined.

Conclusion

I have suggested that there are a number of components which are present in any and every example of interpersonal communication. These components are of course inter-linked as illustrated in the examples:

- features of the social situation influence our social identities
- how we see ourselves influences how we see others - social perception
- these mental or cognitive processes influence how we act - how we encode and decode our communication

Life is further complicated by the fact that all these components can be sub-divided into further processes. For example, your social identity is not a single static entity - it can change and develop and is subject to various influences.

Section B will take each of the four main elements of the model and explore them in more detail.

Notes

1   This definition was first proposed by Harold Lasswell, one of the early American theorists of mass communication, in an article "The Structure and Function of Communication in Society" in the following book:

    L. Bryson, ed (1948) *The Communication of Ideas*, Institute for Religious and Social Studies

2   I have given a rather superficial account of the notion of a theoretical model. Unfortunately it's not quite as simple as that as you will see if you read the following:

    L. Hawes (1975) *Pragmatics of Analoguing: Theory and Model Construction in Communication*, Addison-Wesley

    M. Black (1962) *Models and Metaphors*, Cornell University Press

    S. W. Littlejohn (1983) *Theories of Human Communication*, 2nd edn, Wadsworth

3   As well as this example, Susan Ervin-Tripp has produced many fascinating analyses of the linguistic complexities of everyday speech:

    S. Ervin Tripp (1972) "On Sociolinguistic Rules: Alteration and Co-occurrence", in J. J. Gumperz and D. Hymes, eds, *Directions in Sociolinguistics*, Holt Rinehart and Winston

4   Sociologists who follow the ethnomethodological approach try to discover meanings which we tend to "take-for-granted" in everyday interactions. This example is taken from a leading exponent of this approach:

    H. Garfinkel (1967) *Studies in Ethnomethodology*, Prentice-Hall

5   Taken from Danziger's book referenced in Chapter 1.

3

The skills of interpersonal communication

In this chapter, I shall:

- explain how we can analyse interpersonal communication as skilled behaviour
- explain the main characteristics of the "social skills" model, and suggest important practical implications
- describe and analyse behaviours which are used in the skills of interpersonal communication
- show how these behaviours and skills interrelate, using practical examples
- discuss possible criticisms and limitations of this approach
- relate this skills approach to the model described in Chapter 2

Why should we think of communication as skilled behaviour?

We normally use the term "skill" to refer to physical behaviours (what psychologists call motor skills). We can agree for example that specific sports personalities display certain skills. Ivan Lendl's service in tennis is a pretty formidable piece of behaviour, especially if you are at the receiving end. By using slow motion film or video we can observe his coordination and rhythm, not to mention the power which many other players cannot equal. We can also observe how Lendl varies the shot in order to keep his opponents guessing. In a similar way we can observe a particular social act and try to work out what the participants are doing. And we can observe that some people seem to be far better at handling certain social situations than others. Think of someone whom you like talking to. What do they do to make the conversation enjoyable? They probably make you feel that they really are listening and interested in what you are saying. They do this by giving you encouragement, perhaps smiling, nodding etc. Contrast this picture with someone whom you dislike talking to. What do they do to make it unpleasant? Perhaps they seem to ignore you (the boss who shuffles his papers while insisting that he is listening), or perhaps they try to dominate the proceedings. If you carry on with this sort of analysis you will find that certain behaviours are performed regularly by individuals who are effective or successful in handling social situations and that individuals who are ineffective perform rather differently. And this is the essence of social skills.

To put it another way, Michael Argyle makes the analogy between a motor or physical skill like playing tennis and a social skill like conducting a conversation:[1]

> In each case the performer seeks certain goals, makes skilled moves which are intended to further them, observes what effect he is having and takes corrective action as a result of feedback.

Argyle is one of the major British exponents of this social skills model. Interest in this perspective has grown dramatically in the last ten years in both the UK and USA. The rest of this chapter analyses the social skills model and reviews research on the different behaviours involved.

What is the social skills model?

The model developed by Argyle is probably the most famous summary of the social skills approach - as in the diagram below:[1]

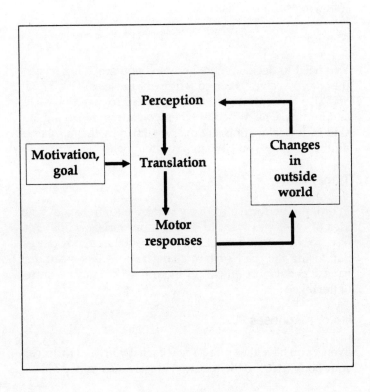

This draws upon the analogy between performance in physical activities and performance in social situations.

You can apply this model very easily to any physical or motor skill. Take the example of riding a bike:

Goal

You can ride a bike for various reasons, ranging from the simple idea of travelling from A to B through to practising elaborate BMX stunts to impress your friends. Having decided your general goal, you will also have more specific objectives, or sub-goals. Whatever the context, one obvious sub-goal is to stay on the bike and avoid falling off. This is the objective you are very conscious of when you are first learning the skill. In order to achieve this you need the following components:

Perception

You need to decide where and how you are going to steer the bike, perceive certain cues from the muscles in your body and also concentrate on the road ahead to avoid obstacles and bumps. One difficulty when you are first learning any skill is the feeling of being overwhelmed by the number of different things you have to pay attention to.

Translation

In order to perform effectively you have to "translate" your idea of what you want to do into appropriate action. You have to choose the correct action to meet the circumstances. Supposing the road surface changes, does this mean you have to pedal more quickly or more slowly to stay in control of the bike?

Motor responses

Even if you have the correct idea of what you need to do, can your body manage the required muscle movements? Have you the strength and power to pedal up that hill which is approaching?

Feedback

If you start to over-balance, do you notice the problem in time to do anything about it? The correct movement (motor response) will bring you back into balance but you need to recognise the effect of what you have done (the feedback loop). If you over-correct your balance then you will fall over the other way.

As we learn a motor skill, our actions become more fluent and better-timed and more of the action becomes sub-conscious - we no longer have to concentrate so hard on keeping balance - our body seems to make automatic adjustments.

How can we apply the social skills model to interpersonal communication?

The same stages seem to apply:

Goals

We have social goals which can also be broken down into subsidiary objectives or sub-goals.
   Suppose I wish to be seen as an interesting lecturer, then I can set myself various sub-goals I need to achieve, including the following:

- assemble material on relevant topics
- use examples and illustrations which are relevant to the audience
- give clear introductions to lectures
- time and pace the material to keep the audience's attention

- present information at the right level to match the audience's experience

I could fail on any or all of the above and have to deal with the sleep-inducing consequences.

Suppose you wish to make friends with someone you have just met, what would you need to do to achieve this goal?

Perception

Suppose you have just been introduced to someone at a party. What do you notice about them? Do they appear happy, relaxed, anxious, nervous, bored or what? If you misjudge their mood you may start the conversation in a way which irritates or antagonises them. Are you looking at their facial expression or gestures or posture? And are you aware of the tone of your voice and your own mannerisms? Are you really giving them a warm welcome?

Translation

Suppose you notice that someone is feeling upset but is not saying anything about it, what do you decide to do? Do you decide to ignore it and pretend all is well or do you think you should encourage them to talk about the problem? If you decide to ask them about it, do you intend to do it directly or adopt a more subtle approach?

Behaviour

You have decided to ask someone what is bothering them - what exactly do you do? What do you say? Do you try to incorporate a gesture which indicates concern like placing a hand on their shoulder?

Feedback

Does the other person interpret your actions in the way you have intended? What if you did place a hand on their shoulder - was this gesture received in the way you intended? Do they respond to your interest as a sincere request or do they react as if you are being too "nosy". If they say "I don't want to talk about it", do you take them at their word? Or do you interpret their reluctance as an invitation to probe further? Do you try again?

How you handle this situation depends on how well you have interpreted their reactions.

What are the implications of this approach?

If we can apply this model to our everyday interactions then we can look at some of its important implications and limitations. First a look at some important implications:

Learning and experience

In the same way that we learn motor skills we have to learn how to behave in social situations. And we may be able to learn from experience how to cope with situations which we find "difficult". Typical examples of situations which many people find difficult are

- situations which demand assertive behaviour, such as complaining to a neighbour about noise or taking faulty goods back to a shop

- situations of great intimacy such as sexual encounters

- situations involving some kind of public performance such as giving a speech

Consider a situation which you once found difficult but now find easier to cope with - what was it like on the first occasion? You were probably very self-conscious and very sensitive to what other people were doing. To use the model's terminology, you were probably concentrating very hard on your goals and trying to appear competent. You were looking hard for feedback to make sure you were behaving appropriately. With experience you become more fluent and you are no longer so self-conscious.

Analysing problems and difficulties

You can explain people's difficulties in social behaviour by using the skills model. It has been extensively used with clinical patients who can have extreme difficulty with everyday situations which most of us take for granted.

On an everyday level, consider the example of "George", a person who sometimes tries to be the life and soul of the party and fails dismally. What goes wrong? There are a number of possibilities suggested by the model:

goals

Perhaps he does not have a clear idea of what he's trying to do and so he behaves inconsistently or erratically?

perception

Perhaps George is not very good at recognising what is going on round him. So he misinterprets the mood of the party and does the wrong thing at the wrong time - perhaps he tells sexist jokes to a group who find such humour offensive.

translation into behaviour

Perhaps George can understand what to do but cannot put it into practice. He knows the jokes but his sense of timing is so poor that he ruins the punch lines.

feedback

Perhaps George does not clearly recognise how the other party guests react to him. If he gets a good response from the first joke he probably launches into a long routine and ignores the increasing signs of boredom from his audience. Like the compulsive gambler, he does not recognise when to stop.

Careful observation of George's behaviour along with discussion of his aims and feelings could highlight which of these problems is the actual one.

You can teach or train social skills

There is now considerable evidence that you can successfully train people to improve their social skills. The success of the training depends upon how well-defined the skills are and the quality of the training. I have made this sound very simple and straightforward. In fact the issue of training in social and communication skills is complex for a number of reasons:

social skills are not just like motor skills
I shall discuss this in more detail below

social skills can be quite difficult to specify
It can be difficult to specify exactly the behaviours which are the necessary components of a particular social skill. This is not altogether surprising as people have different styles of behaviour which can be equally successful.

there are different training methods available
For example, one recent book[2] distinguishes methods based upon:

- thinking (using lectures and discussions)
- feeling (focussing upon the participants' feelings and emotional reactions)
- doing (using case-studies and role-plays)

The authors then go on to outline yet another method which tries to integrate these different approaches.

it is difficult to measure the outcomes of training
It is difficult to measure changes in people's behaviour.[3] Even if you find that someone's behaviour has changed it

41

may not be the direct result of the training - perhaps other people are treating them differently.

the success of training may depend as much on the personal qualities of the trainer as on the training method
Changing your behaviour can be a nerve-racking experience. A lot will depend upon the level of trust between the trainer and client.

Despite these difficulties there is now significant support for the effectiveness of training based on social skill principles.[4]

Motor skills are not the same as social skills

The social skills model can be applied in useful ways but it is also important not to lose sight of the fact that social skills are unlike motor skills in many important ways:[5]

Other people have goals
In motor skills you are dealing with inert objects. Barring accidents, my bike is under my control and goes where I direct it. I do not have to worry about its aims and intentions. In social situations, the other participants also have goals. If I wish to dominate you and you wish to dominate me, then we are preparing for battle and not constructive dialogue.

The importance of feelings
To quote Argyle:[6]

> A cyclist is not constantly wondering how the bicycle is feeling, or whether it thinks he is riding it nicely.

In developing a motor skill such as playing snooker you have to deal with materials and equipment which do not react or have feelings. This is very different in social skills. You cannot predict the reactions of other people in the same way that you can predict that a snooker ball will stop dead if you hit the stun shot correctly.

Metaperception

As well as directly perceiving our own behaviour and the behaviour of others, we can also reflect on how those other people are perceiving us. This has been called "meta-perception"[7] and has been shown to be an important factor in determining how people react to one another. For example, if we are having a conversation and I get the impression that you think I am being too "chatty" then I might become more reserved to counteract this impression. If my initial impression is wrong then I will probably confuse you or even offend you with my sudden and unexplained change in behaviour.

Situation and personal factors

As explained later in this book we make all sorts of judgements about the other people we communicate with and the situation we are in. Even though these judgements can be subconscious they will affect how we communicate.

Some of these complexities will become more apparent as we look at the behaviours which make up our interpersonal skills.

What are the components of interpersonal skills?

I shall discuss specific skills as they crop up later in the book but some examples will illustrate the general approach.

One typical and comprehensive text[8] on interpersonal communication skills included the following topics:

- nonverbal communication (NVC)
- reinforcement
- questioning

- reflecting
- opening and closing
- explanation
- listening
- self-disclosure

Many of these headings are reasonably self-explanatory but more detailed descriptions will provide a fuller introduction to social skills analysis:

Nonverbal communication

Nonverbal communication (NVC for short) or bodily communication[9] is usually taken to mean a range of nonverbal signals, which includes the following:

- facial expression
- gaze
- gestures
- posture
- bodily contact
- spatial behaviour
- clothes and appearance
- nonverbal vocalisations
- smell

As these comprise some of the most significant codes we use, I shall discuss them in some detail in Chapter 7.

Reinforcement

This refers to behaviours which encourage the other person to carry on or repeat whatever they happen to be doing. Various experiments have shown the reinforcing influence of expressions of praise, encouragement, and support, even down to the use of head nods, grunts and the "uh-huh". A simple laboratory experiment which illustrated this process was described as follows:[10]

> Subjects in this study were simply asked to produce as many individual words as they could think of. Each occasion on which a plural noun was given, the experimenter responded with "mm-hmm" while all other types of words were largely ignored. It was found that gradually the number of cases of plural nouns increased substantially.

Questioning

If you have attended a series of job interviews you will know that some professional interviewers are much better than others at extracting information from you. This will be due in part to their question technique - whether they are asking the right sort of question at the right time. For example, texts on interviewing technique[11] usually distinguish between open and closed questions. An open question allows the person to answer in whatever way they like, eg what do you think of John Major? A closed question asks for specific information or a yes/no response, eg do you agree with John Major's economic policy? Open questions encourage people to talk and expand; closed questions encourage short answers. Inexperienced interviewers often ask too many closed questions and do not get the elaborated answers which they really want.

Reflecting

This is a skill often used by counsellors and other people who have to conduct very personal interviews and who want the other person to talk in some detail about their own feelings and attitudes. Questions can often direct the conversation in ways which reflect the interviewer's assumptions so it can be more revealing to use reflections which feedback to the speaker some aspect of what they have just said. This acts as a cue for them to elaborate or extend what they have been saying. You can reflect in different ways and achieve different results. This will depend on whether you are interested in the factual statements that the other person has made or their feelings about what they are saying.

The following alternative versions of an imaginary conversation illustrate different forms of reflections and different reactions which they may achieve:

Keywords
This involves the listener identifying a key word or phrase which will encourage the speaker to say more:

A: "I have travelled quite a lot over the years and I always enjoy travelling. I did most of it when I worked for ICL."

B: "ICL?"

A: "Yes, I worked there for five years up until the time..."

B chose a keyword in what A had said and simply repeated it. A recognised this as a signal to elaborate on this and the conversation develops.

Paraphrasing
This involves the listener summarising what they have heard in their own words.

A: "I have travelled quite a lot over the years and I always enjoy travelling. I did most of it when I worked for ICL."

B: "So you have done a lot of travelling."

A: "Yes, I suppose I must have visited all the major countries in Europe and ..."

Here B gave a brief summary or paraphrasing of what he had just heard. Again A took this as a cue to develop the conversation in a particular way.

Reflecting feeling

This is where the listener identifies the feelings which the speaker implies in the way they talk.

A "I have travelled quite a lot over the years and I always enjoy travelling. I did most of it when I worked for ICL."

B : "You sound as though you wished you were still doing a lot of travelling."

A : "Yes I do miss it a lot and I wish there was ..."

Here B has probably focussed on the way A spoke. Perhaps A talked with a hint of regret in his tone of voice. By accurately spotting this and using a reflection B has enabled A to express some of his feelings.

This last form of reflection is perhaps the most difficult and most skilful - you have to sense the underlying emotion accurately and read between the lines. Often quite subtle clues are involved. Consider the following statement:

"I worked in the packing department at Hill's. All I did from nine o'clock until five was put tins into cardboard boxes, day after day after day."

This straightforward description of a job gives several clear clues to the underlying emotion. The phrases "all I did" and "day after day" combine to convey the atmosphere of routine and boredom.[12]

Opening and closing

This refers to the ways in which we establish the beginnings and endings of a particular interaction. For example, sales staff often receive very detailed training on how to start the interaction with the customer. Often this involves making conversation to establish the sales representative as more friendly and helpful than "just a salesman". Consider all the different possible ways of starting a conversation with someone - some ways would be much more appropriate than others in particular circumstances.

The choice of opening can be very important in more formal situations such as an interview where the opening can establish either a positive or negative atmosphere. There are a number of ways to start an interview, including the following three:[13]

social opening

The interviewer makes sure to give the interviewee a positive welcome and spends some time in social conversation - breaking the ice - before getting down to business.

factual opening

The interviewer starts with a clear description of important facts, perhaps by explaining how they see their role, or explaining how they see the goals of the interview, or by summarising what has happened previously.

motivational opening

The interviewer starts with an attempt to encourage and motivate the interviewee perhaps by introducing some visual aid or gadget to stimulate interest.

There is also a similar variety of tactics available to close or conclude an interaction. The good interviewer will make sure that the interviewee has a chance to clear up any points they have not understood and will make sure that they know what is going to happen as a result of the interview.

Listening

It may seem odd to regard listening as a skill but that is because we tend to think of it as a passive activity rather than being an activity we have to concentrate on and work at. In fact there has now been considerable research into how we listen to each other and this research has identified important factors:

- typical problems or barriers to effective listening

- different patterns of listening behaviour

- behaviours which seem to help the other person express themselves and which therefore help us listen to them

Typical listening barriers

Some problems are fairly obvious - problems caused by external distractions or lack of interest. Other problems are more subtle such as verbal battling or fact hunting:[14]

verbal battle
This is the situation where, instead of listening and absorbing what the other person has to say, we start to debate the ideas in our own head and come up with counter-arguments or criticisms. While we do this we lose track of the other points the person is making.

fact hunting
Instead of listening for the main theme or general points in the argument we concentrate on the detailed facts and lose sight of the overall message.

If you identify these problems you can overcome them. Attempts to train people to become better listeners typically try to get people to identify these "bad habits". For example, we can think much faster than we speak and this can either help us listen or add to the distractions: [14]

The differential between thought speed and speech rate may encourage the listener to fill up the spare time with other unrelated thought processes (such as day-dreaming), which in turn may distract the listener from assimilating the speaker's message. Listening can be improved by using this spare thought-time positively, by asking covert questions

49

such as: "What are the main points being expressed by the speaker?" ; "What reasons are being given?" ; "In what frame of reference should these reasons be taken?" ; and "What further information is necessary?"

Patterns and styles of listening

Sometimes someone appears to be listening to you but you suspect they are not:

pretend listeners
They appear to be attentive and are making some appropriate nonverbal signals but their minds are elsewhere.

limiting listeners
They only give limited attention to what you are saying - they are focussing on specific topics or comments and may distort or misinterpret other things you say.

self-centred listeners
They are only really concerned with their own views and may be simply looking for your agreement.

Talking to someone who exhibits one of these styles can be very frustrating.

Positive or active listening
Good listening is often described as active listening - not only do you have to internally absorb and process the information you receive but you also have to encourage the other person to talk and demonstrate clearly that you are paying attention. As a result, some authors have sub-divided listening into more specific clusters of skills, such as:[15]

- attending skills

- following skills

- reflecting skills

The behaviours which seem to be associated with effective listening involve both bodily communication and internal thinking. Typical recommendations include:[16]

- being receptive to the other person - showing that you are prepared to listen and accept what they are saying (of course, this does not mean that you automatically agree with it). Nonverbal signals are obviously important here and you need to avoid any signs of tension or impatience.

- maintaining attention - using eye contact, head nods, and appropriate facial expression

- removing distractions

- delaying evaluation of what you have heard until you fully understand it

Self-disclosure

When you communicate with other people you tell them various things about yourself. Sidney Jourard coined the term "self-disclosure" to refer to the process of sharing information about ourselves with other people.[17] So when you self-disclose, you reveal to the other person some aspect of how you feel. Jourard was interested in how people came to reveal aspects of themselves to others and how this process influenced the development of good personal relationships. Perhaps the best way of visualising the process is using a diagram known as the Johari Window - so-called after its two originators, Joe Luft and Harry Ingham.[18]

The window categorises information that you and others have about yourself into four segments:

Open	Blind
Hidden	Unknown

Open
This contains information about myself which I know and which others know about me, eg the fact that I am married with two children.

Hidden
This is information which I know about myself and which I am not prepared to reveal to other people, eg specific fears and anxieties which I may feel a bit embarrassed about and which are certainly not going to be published here.

Blind
This is information which others know about me and which I am not aware of, eg annoying habits which I do not notice in myself. This blind area can contain very important information - if I see myself as a considerate and approachable leader and others see me as domineering and aggressive then this will inevitably lead to problems.

Unknown
This information is not known to me or others at present but may surface at some future point, eg I may have some very deep-rooted unconscious anxieties which are currently well under control.

When I self-disclose I enlarge the open segment and decrease the other segments. If I receive feedback from others then I can also increase my open segment and decrease my blind segment.

There are several practical implications of self-disclosure, the most important being its effect on our relationships:

Self-disclosure and relationships

In order to initiate a relationship with someone, you need to self-disclose. What do you tell the other person? How soon do you reveal more personal feelings? Your answer to these questions may well determine how the relationship develops. We are suspicious of other people who become "too personal too soon".[19]

This issue of how much information we reveal to others is a very real problem for some professional groups. If you are a social worker and a client explains personal feelings which you can identify with, do you share your experience with the client or do you maintain a more neutral stance?

Conclusion

This account of all the different behaviours which can contribute to skilled performance may seem a rather daunting list. Of course, all of these behaviours are not relevant or appropriate in every situation. You can expect different patterns of behaviour in different situations - for example, in a job interview the interviewer is likely to concentrate on questioning; in a counselling interview, the interviewer is likely to do much more reflecting and reinforcing.

The socially skilled person is the person who can choose the appropriate behaviours to suit the situation they are in, and then perform these behaviours in an appropriate combination and sequence. Of course, this makes it sound rather too easy - some of the complexities are revealed in the next chapter when we look at how social skills can work (or not) in everyday life.

Notes

1   This model is taken from Michael Argyle, one of the pioneers of this approach in the UK. Starting from his early publications in the 1960s, he has produced a series of books and articles on social skills, including perhaps the best-known paperback introduction to social behaviour, now in its 4th edition, which uses the model explained in this chapter:

    M. Argyle and A. Kendon (1967) "The Experimental Analysis of Social Performance", in L. Berkowitz, ed, *Advances in Experimental Social Psychology*, Academic Press

    M. Argyle (1983) *The Psychology of Interpersonal Behaviour*, 4th edn, Penguin

2   As well as providing their own approach, the authors offer interesting comments on other methods:

    N. Clark, K. Phillips and D. Barker (1984) *Unfinished Process*, Gower Press

3   For an example of how this is studied, see the chapter by Marzillir in:

    P. Trower, B. Bryant and M. Argyle, eds (1978) *Social Skills and Mental Health*, Methuen

4   For further analysis of this debate, and more comprehensive discussion of social skills, see the books by Owen Hargie and his colleagues:

    O. Hargie, C. Saunders and D. Dickson (1981 and 1989) *Social Skills in Interpersonal Communication*, 1st and 2nd editions, Croom Helm

    O. Hargie, ed (1988) *Handbook of Communication Skills*, Croom Helm

5   See the discussion in Argyle, 1983, op cit.

6   Argyle, 1983, op cit.

7   For a discussion of the practical implications of this and other forms of "meta-communication", see:

L. Porritt (1990) *Interaction Strategies*, 2nd edn, Churchill Livingstone

8   This list is taken from Hargie et al. (1981) op cit. In the second edition, they added chapters on assertiveness and small groups which are discussed later in this book.

9   For a comprehensive survey of recent research into NVC see:

M. Argyle (1988) *Bodily Communication*, 2nd edn, Methuen

10   See the discussion in Hargie et al., p 77f

11   For example, see the section on interview question technique in Chapter 4 of:

P. L. Wright and D. S. Taylor (1984) *Improving Leadership Performance*, Prentice Hall

12   See the article by Saunders in Hargie, 1988 edn.

13   For a detailed analysis of interviewer tactics and skills, see Chapters 6 and 7 of:

R. Miller, V. Crute and O. Hargie (1992) *Professional Interviewing*, Routledge

14   See p 130ff in:

M. Ruffner and M. Burgoon (1981) *Interpersonal Communication*, Holt, Rinehart and Winston

15   For a detailed analysis of these skills, see:

R. Bolton (1987) *People Skills*, Simon Schuster

16   For an interesting book which discusses both training and self-help aspects of relationship skills, see Nelson-Jones. For a recent and typical summary of the practical implications of listening, see Hayes:

R. Nelson-Jones (1986) *Human Relationship Skills*, Cassell

J. Hayes (1991) *Interpersonal Skills*, Harper Collins

17 There has now been considerable research on this topic since the original text:

S. M. Jourard (1971) *Self-disclosure*, Wiley

18 The window is explained in considerable detail in:

J. Luft (1970) *Group Processes*, 2nd edn, National Press Books

19 For a typical discussion, see:

S. Duck (1977) *The Study of Acquaintance*, Gower

4

Communication skills in context

In this chapter I shall

- analyse a series of practical examples which illustrate how the social skills model can be applied

- review criticisms and possible limitations of this approach

- relate the social skills approach to the model of interpersonal communication outlined in Chapter 2

Practical examples of communication skills at work (or not!)

We become most aware of social skills in everyday life when they "break down", ie when someone blunders and displays some deficiency in their level of skills. So to illustrate the workings of communication skills I shall use examples which range from the fairly light-hearted to the very serious:

- Fred at parties
- Chairing a meeting
- The nurse's diagnosis

Fred at parties

In my college days I had a friend who used to create problems at parties. He was very susceptible to alcohol. After a couple of drinks his social skills deteriorated. Unfortunately his enthusiasm for social interaction seemed to rise in direct proportion to his intake of alcohol. And this caused the problems.

In his enthusiastic/inebriated state, Fred would adopt a particular style of interaction. He would stand very close to people, talk at them very animatedly and would stare them straight in the eye all the time. This combination of behaviour was interpreted by males as "aggressive and/or suspicious" and by females as "too pushy and too macho too soon". His group of friends had to rescue him at regular intervals before his victims decided to turn the tables.

The irony in this tale is that Fred would never understand why he was so unsuccessful at parties and we, his friends, could never bring ourselves to tell him in case it hurt his feelings. We could never think of a way of explaining the problem which would help Fred to do something about it. Our subtle attempts to wean him off alcohol all failed. He felt that a couple of pints built up his confidence and did not recognise that this increased confidence was having such a disastrous effect. He was also very anxious to be "one of the lads" and show that he could cope with alcohol in the same way that most of us thought we could.

How could the social skills approach have helped Fred? At the very least, a short burst of social skills training with special emphasis on nonverbal communication would have helped Fred both to understand what he was doing and to appreciate the effect he was creating with his behaviour style. But would this be sufficient? Having recognised the problem could he then resist the temptation to have a few pints before the party? And how confident would he be without the false confidence induced by alcohol? Again social skills training could help. Presumably Fred lacked confidence because he was unsure of how to behave. How do you strike up a conversation with someone at a party in a convincing way? Social skills training could have analysed Fred's present strategies and suggested alternatives which would build his self-confidence.

This very brief example may seem rather trivial but several surveys have found that many people have difficulty with everyday social situations and this can cause considerable anxiety and loneliness.[1] This example also suggests some of the complexities of social skills analysis - to do it properly you need a lot of information on the person's behaviour and feelings as well as a clear knowledge of the situations which create difficulty.

Chairing a meeting

Most people have attended at least one committee meeting which was chaired badly - perhaps the meeting went on and on without seeming to get anywhere, perhaps the decisions were pushed through without sufficient discussion, perhaps the participants interrupted each other and spoke at cross-purposes. These problems should not occur if the meeting is being chaired efficiently. But what counts as efficient or skilful behaviour in this context?

Despite the pervasiveness of meetings in everyday life and work, there is very little research on what chairpersons actually do. There are several books offering advice but these tend to be based on the authors' personal experience rather than any systematic research.[2] However there is one systematic study which highlights what a good chairperson actually does.[3]

This research also highlights some of the main difficulties in research in social skills -

- identifying the measure of success, competence or effectiveness

- making valid observations of the actual behaviour

- identifying effective behaviour

As the authors comment:

Apart from satisfaction measures, and these can be misleading, it is difficult to specify the performance criteria which indicate an expert chairman. The measures sometimes used in training evaluation, such as the time taken to complete the meeting or the number of decisions reached per hour, seemed to us naive and inappropriate.

The main criteria used in the research were participants' ratings of fairness and efficiency in conjunction with the experience of the chairman himself (all the subjects were male). The behaviour of chairmen who received the highest ratings were compared with the behaviour of other people in the meeting. Important differences emerged as we shall see later.

Observing behaviour

In order to make a systematic analysis of what someone is doing we need a method of observation. In other words, we need some sort of classification system. The most popular system used by researchers over the years is the system first proposed by Robert Bales.[4] His Interaction Process Analysis uses twelve categories. Every act is classified in one of the categories. Of course every time someone speaks they can perform several acts:

The twelve behaviour categories in Interaction Process Analysis are given below (see footnote 4 for references which provide a more detailed description of the IPA categories and their development):

Shows solidarity
Shows tension release
Agrees
Gives suggestion
Gives opinion
Gives orientation
Asks for orientation
Asks for opinion
Asks for suggestion
Disagrees
Shows tension
Shows antagonism

An example may make this clearer :

"OK, but can we hang on a bit. I think we should proceed very slowly. And I'd like to hear what Jane thinks."

This contains four acts:

- OK - shows agreement

- but can we hang on a bit - gives suggestion

- I think we should proceed very slowly - gives suggestion

- And I'd like to hear what Jane thinks - asks for suggestion

Having experimented with this classification and other examples, Rackham and Morgan[3] concluded that different contexts needed rather different classifications depending on what you were interested in. For example, chairing a

61

meeting involves controlling the participation of the members, either bringing people in to make a contribution or cutting them off. These behaviours are not directly registered in Bales' system. So Rackham and Morgan developed their own systems for particular studies, working from a general purpose set of the following categories. The thirteen categories group into four broader categories - initiating, reacting, clarifying and controlling participation:

Initiating

- Proposing
- Building

Reacting

- Supporting
- Disagreeing
- Defending/attacking
- Blocking/difficulty-stating

Clarifying

- Open
- Testing understanding
- Summarising
- Seeking information
- Giving information

Controlling participation

- Shutting out
- Bringing in

They tested this system to make sure that observers could use it reliably. A classification system is of little help if observers find it difficult to use or if different observers arrive at very different interpretations of the same behaviour.

Other researchers have also developed observation schemes for particular situations. For example, Flanders has developed a scheme for classroom interaction[5] which focusses on the different ways that teachers behave in order to control their pupils.

The effective chair

Applying the observation scheme in a series of meetings led to a series of conclusions. There was no doubt that the chairmen who were regarded as effective behaved very differently from chairmen who were rated as less effective. And effective chairmen behaved very differently from other members of the meeting - to quote a couple of examples:[3]

Testing understanding. One of the most significant differences between chairmen and members was the very high level of testing understanding (15.2 per cent) in the chairmen, compared with 3.1 per cent from group members. Testing understanding, like summarizing, allows a retrospective control of what has been said. It organizes and ties down previous points and people's understanding of them.

Summarizing. The difference here (12.5 per cent for chairman, 0.7 per cent for meeting members) is the greatest on any category. This emphasizes how strongly associated summarizing is with the role of chairman. The association is so strong that if another member of the meeting attempts to summarize, this is frequently seen as a personal challenge to the chairman and his authority.

Other differences included:

- more procedural proposals
- less supporting behaviour (remaining neutral and not expressing support for particular ideas)
- less disagreeing (again this was associated with the desire to remain neutral)
- much more information-seeking, but less information-giving

Thus this research did develop a clear specification for the behaviour associated with effective chairmanship, although the authors are careful to point out that their findings might be specific to the context they investigated. Different types of organisation or different types of groups could demand different combinations of behaviour in skilled chairpersons. And remember again that this study was only concerned with male subjects.

In the context of this investigation, the specification could be used to evaluate the behaviour of the individual chair and also as a basis for training. Training would be based on the following stages:

Diagnosis: an individual's behaviour is categorised using the specification from the research

Feedback: the individual is given feedback on how they are doing

Practice: the individual is given time to practice and work on improvements

The nurse's diagnosis

This example is taken from an article by Peter Maguire[6] where he analyses the following patient assessment which was produced by an experienced nurse. Colostomy involves surgery which creates an artificial opening in the wall of the abdomen so waste is discharged through this opening into a "bag" which the patient has to change at regular intervals.

Mrs T is a 54 year old married woman with three grown-up children. She had a colostomy for rectal cancer four months ago. She called in at the clinic to see me because she was having trouble with her bag. It had been leaking and causing an offensive smell. She had stopped going out much because of it. Otherwise she appears to be coping well. I've given her a new bag and will call on her in a week's time to see how she is getting on.

This assessment suggests that Mrs T is having difficulties of a fairly practical nature. A very different picture emerged by an independent assessment. This revealed that Mrs T had a number of other problems:

- she had serious sexual problems
- she had become very depressed
- she was sleeping badly and had little energy
- she was feeling both helpless and hopeless

So why did this experienced nurse miss these points? Her next assessment was recorded and analysed. Several problems in communication skills emerged. For example:

opening

The nurse would start with a comment like "I'm here to see if you have been having any problems with your stoma". She failed to make her role explicit. This rather abrupt opening made the patient feel that the nurse was only interested in any practical problems she was experiencing with her bag. As a result, the patient did not feel she could express her more fundamental problems as this would take too much time and was not appropriate. Of course the nurse would have been very willing to explore these problems if they had emerged.

questioning

The nurse did not use open questions which would have invited the patient to speak out like "how's your stoma been?" Instead she asked leading questions like "Your stoma's been working well, hasn't it?" which encourage short answers.

listening

The nurse was failing to notice signs of worry and distress in the patient's answers. For example:

> When the nurse began by asking "Your stoma's been working well, hasn't it?" the patient said "Well, yes, I suppose it has, but I've been a bit worried sometimes ... ". The nurse seized on the "suppose it has" and rightly checked that the stoma and bag were all right. She failed to acknowledge the cue "worried".

This example illustrates a problem which confronts many people occupying professional roles in society - nurses, doctors, lawyers, policemen etc. Their judgements and decisions can have a dramatic effect on other people's lives. Most of their information is derived from interpersonal communication. So the quality of their decision depends upon their communication skills. And yet they receive very little training in this area. We can hardly blame the nurse for poor questioning technique if she has never been trained in it. Many professional groups are now looking at communication skills very seriously but there is still a long way to go before they are given the attention they deserve. Two recent quotes relating to the medical profession illustrate this point:[7]

> Many health care professionals (including nurses) feel that the ... interpersonal issues involved in practitioner-patient interactions are naturally and automatically understood and acted upon. Many practitioners believe that interpersonal issues do not require active concern and scientific study.

> ... there is still a common belief that socially skilled action and methods of interpersonal relating are not

amenable to training or education. It is still common to hear nurses at all levels say that social skills just come naturally.

Are there any limitations to the social skills approach?

The social skills approach, and social skills training in particular, has been criticised on a number of counts. There are four lines of criticism that have important implications for this book:

Mechanical nature?

Does the skills approach present an over-mechanical and almost "demeaning" view of human interaction?

Perhaps some texts have created a misleading impression by implying that we all behave very mechanically, and that there are very definite techniques which always achieve certain social results. But this is not the impression you will receive from the more recent and more sophisticated texts.[8] These emphasise the complex nature of human interaction, and also examine a broader set of issues than the specific behaviours involved. Which leads on to the second question:

Cognitive factors?

Does the social skills approach ignore the way we think and feel (cognitive and emotional factors) and concentrate too much on the observed behaviour?

Admittedly Argyle's model does talk about goals and purposes. But are there other factors which are important? You can possess a skill without actually using it - you may not believe that you can perform effectively and so you refuse to try. So a person may actually be able to behave in a skilled manner but may not do so because they lack self-confidence, ie they feel that they will be unsuccessful. The importance of a person's feelings and beliefs cannot be ignored and these issues have now been recognised as an important area within the social skills approach.

Social context?

Does social skills analysis ignore the social context?

Again this is an issue that is being given increasing attention by social skills researchers [9]. As we shall see in Chapter 5, the social context exerts strong influences on our behaviour. Behaviour that is seen as appropriate in one context will not necessarily be so in another.

Social skills and etiquette?

Does social skills analysis have a hidden political dimension - does it represent a strict adherence to the status quo?

Following this line of argument, some critics have suggested that social skills training is highly prescriptive and not as neutral or as scientific as it claims to be:[10]

> The social skills trainer therefore displaces the book on etiquette, which itself eventually replaced the code of chivalry.

The force of this criticism really depends on how social skills approach relates to other knowledge we have of our social behaviour. And that leads me to the final topic of this chapter - how does the social skills approach relate to the model of interpersonal communication?

Social skills and the model of interpersonal communication

- interpersonal communication is an ongoing process with several inter-related components

- whenever people communicate they behave in particular ways which are more or less successful in achieving their goals

These two sentences reflect the two different approaches which have been described so far. Are these two incompatible ways of understanding interpersonal communication? I do not think so - they must be seen as complementary perspectives. The analysis of ongoing processes must contain reference to the specific behaviours involved - the analysis of skilled behaviour must always look beyond the specific behaviour in order to understand its true significance.

Some practical examples may make this point clearer:

Goals and meaning

The social skills approach suggests that people pursue goals in social situations. These goals may not be totally shared by participants in an interaction. For example Argyle[11] suggests that nurses and patients regard the following goals as the most important when they interact:

Nurse

- mutual acceptance
- taking care of other
- looking after self

Patient

- mutual acceptance
- obtaining information
- own well-being

There is an interesting potential source of conflict here - the patient wants information, the nurse does not see that as an important goal. The nurse's notion of "taking care" may exclude any possibility of exchanging information. If patients make repeated attempts to "quiz" the nurse this may cause conflict as the nurse remains unforthcoming. Frustration is likely to build up on both sides - patients become irritated as their goal remains unsatisfied; the nurse becomes frustrated as this constant battle of wits distracts from the major goal of taking care.

But what is important about these goals is not just their implications for specific interactions. These goals represent particular role definitions which have developed in a particular society at a particular point in time. Would patients in previous generations have been so anxious to find out more information? Would they not have placed much greater reliance and trust in the doctors, and perhaps not even seen the nurses as a source of information? Changes in society and the spread of information have weakened the power of medical authority. Patients are much less accepting of conventional medical advice, the growth of alternative medicine being one example of this shift. Of course this more critical tendency will be much more pronounced in certain groups of patients. The percentage of patient-nurse relationships which involve real conflict over goals is probably very small.

The general point I am making here is that the meaning of particular behaviours always involves some consideration of broader features of the situation in which the behaviours occur. So any understanding of skilled behaviour also depends upon a sophisticated analysis of the situation in which it occurs. The social skill approach must depend upon our theories and models of communication or it will descend into rather mechanical rules of etiquette. To analyse behaviours and skills we need models of social situations - to develop models we need to investigate the detailed units of interaction.

The case of the skiiing student

To provide one further illustration of how different levels of analysis can complement each other we can use a situation described by Gorden.[12]

Our student, Bob, has just been invited to join a skiing weekend with some friends. The offer of free transport and accommodation seem too good to miss but it will mean returning to college too late for the Monday morning lecture. College rules do not demand that students report absences but Ben decides to make some attempt to find out what will be in the lecture in advance so he can make up the work. He also wants to stay on good terms with the tutor. He goes to the tutor's office and the conversation starts like this:

"Hello Dr Belden! Could I speak to you for a minute?"

"Surely"

"I was just wondering if anything important will be going on in class on Monday."

"Why do you ask?"

"Well, to be frank, I have a chance to take a skiing trip this weekend, and I wanted to find out if I would be missing anything."

If we interrupt the interaction at this point we find an annoyed Dr Belden and a rather confused Bob, who has not anticipated that his request would cause any antagonism. How do we explain these reactions? And how could Bob have handled it differently?

Bob obviously did not recognise certain important details which were significant in this conversation:

- the subtle innuendos in his second question - the mention of "anything important" clearly suggests that this class occurs on occasion without anything important happening. This is the first blow to Dr Belden's professional status.

- the question which raised a question - Bob's question was answered by a question. We do accept that higher status people have a right to do this but it immediately suggests some suspicion towards the first question.

71

- his response to the D's question - he repeated the idea of "missing anything" and did not give the tutor any information which the tutor would find positive - he did not express any desire to catch up with the work, only enthusiasm at the prospective trip - further blows to the tutor's profession.

These are points which you could expect from a social skills analysis. However they only make sense because of all the social knowledge which we take for granted. Dr Belden's reactions relate to his view of himself as strongly committed to his subject matter and working hard to transform students like Bob into competent and hardworking scholars in an institution which sets fairly high standards. Bob's rather dismissive comments on the Monday class are a blow to his individual efforts as a tutor, and to his subject area, and to the more general philosophy of the organisation. So the specific behaviours only make sense when you have a fuller account of the social situation. A different organisational setting would bring different reactions - in a college with a more relaxed attitude to class work, the typical staff attitude would probably be different.

How could Bob have handled this situation differently? Suppose instead of the first question, he had said:

"I am afraid I may miss your lecture next Monday morning and I'd like your advice on how I can catch up on the work."

This avoids the innuendos - would it achieve a more positive reaction?

Conclusion

Perhaps the most important conclusion that emerges from looking at examples of communication skills in action is that we can identify behaviours which are effective in enabling people to understand each other in particular situations.

And this also suggests a point that social skills trainers would wish to emphasise - there is no magic box of tricks which you can apply to each and every situation and guarantee effective communication. Deciding what behaviour will be effective involves a detailed understanding of the participants and their social context. And this is why we need both theoretical understanding *and* practical analysis of interpersonal communication.

Notes

1   Peter Trower and colleagues provide a survey of
     social skills' deficiency in both psychiatric and non-
     psychiatric contexts in:

     P. Trower, B. Bryant and M. Argyle (1978) *Social Skills
     and Mental Health*, Methuen

2   For a typical example, see p 115ff of:

     G. Wells (1986) *How to Communicate*, 2nd edn,
     McGraw-Hill

3   This example is taken from a fascinating book by
     Rackham and Morgan where they describe how they
     developed and refined techniques for observing how
     people behave in work situations:

     N. Rackham and T. Morgan (1977) *Behaviour
     Analysis in Training*, McGraw-Hill

4   Bales originally described IPA in his 1950 book. He
     revised and updated it in the 1970 book but most
     summaries rely on the 1950 presentation. There are
     summaries of the system and its applications in vir-
     tually every general textbook on social psychology -
     see Pennington for a recent British example.

     R. F. Bales (1950) *Interaction Process Analysis: A Method
     for the Study of Small Groups*, Addison-Wesley

     R. F. Bales (1970) *Personality and Interpersonal
     Behaviour*, Holt Rinehart and Winston

     D. C. Pennington (1986) *Essential Social Psychology*,
     Edward Arnold

5   For a recent discussion of the implications of this
     approach, see:

     N. A. Flanders (1991) "Human Interaction Models of
     Teaching", in K. Marjoribanks, ed, *The Foundations of
     Students' Learning*, Pergamon

6   Maguire's article appears in the book edited by Carolyn Kagan, which is well worth reading even if you are not specifically interested in the nursing profession:

C. M. Kagan, ed (1985) *Interpersonal Skills in Nursing*, Croom Helm

7   These two quotes introduce the article by Peter Bannister and Carolyn Kagan on "The Need for Research into Interpersonal Skills in Nursing", in the book by Kagan op cit.

8   To illustrate the complexity and the sophistication of modern approaches - one recent handbook runs to two volumes, 565 pages and over 1800 references:

C. R. Hollin and P. Trower, eds (1986) *Handbook of Social Skills Training*, Pergamon

9   See the article by Colin Davidson on "The Theoretical Antecedents to Social Skills Training", in Kagan op cit.

10 Alan Radley expands on this criticism in the article:

A. Radley (1985) "From Courtesy to Strategy: Some Old Developments", *Bulletin of British Psychological Society*, 38, 209-211

11 It is also worth considering the notion of rules in analysing interactions like this. Argyle discusses doctor and patient rules on p 271ff of:

M. Argyle and M. Henderson (1985) *The Anatomy of Relationships*, Penguin

12 Gorden's text offers a very detailed analysis of the skills of interviewing:

R. L. Gorden (1987) *Interviewing: Strategies, Techniques, and Tactics*, 4th edn, Dorsey Press

Section B

Understanding the components of interpersonal communication

5

The social context

In this chapter, I shall

- discuss the meaning and significance of the social context

- define and discuss each of the components of the social context.

- discuss how these components interact with one another, using examples from research into the relationships we have with others

- discuss the way these components develop over time, again using examples from research into personal relationships

What is the social context and how does it affect communication?

If you read any number of recent texts about human communication, you will probably find a strong emphasis on the social aspects of communication. Authors are very insistent that "communication is a social process"[1] and that communication always takes place within a given society at a given time. But what does this actually mean when we come to try to analyse communication?

You can quite easily find examples of messages which will be interpreted very differently depending on who is receiving them and at what time. For example, the following headline in a national newspaper was read as a straightforward announcement of army tactics in 1943. Nowadays people tend to read rather more colourful connotations into it:

8th Army Push Bottles Up Jerries.

One reason why modern authors place a strong emphasis on the social context is simply because early authors tended to neglect it. For example, there is little concern for the social context in the early models of communication which concentrated on Encoder-Channel-Decoder propositions.

There is also something of a battle which is carried on within the social sciences between those who regard society as the backdrop against which humans choose to act and those who feel that society creates or determines the ways in which we act. If you follow the first viewpoint then you are likely to believe that there are features of human experience which are universal or common to all races and cultures. If you follow the latter viewpoint then you are likely to believe that all human action is relative to the society in which it occurs, ie that there are no universal features of human nature or experience. These arguments may seem very abstract or remote but you will find that they do have very concrete practical implications. For example, communication between different cultures depends on the different cultures being able to develop a common understanding. If all experience is relative to your own culture then this communication could be impossible.[2]

I have over-simplified this argument simply because I have not the space to explore it fully.[3] If you want to put me on the spot for an opinion then I will argue that there are some aspects of human experience which are virtually universal. If this was not the case then communication would be impossible. On the other hand I also maintain that you cannot fully understand any process of human communication without understanding the social context in which it occurs.

But if I simply say that communication is affected by the social context then that does not take us very far. What we need is a more systematic definition of the social context:

- what are the relevant components?
- what are the specific factors which affect us?
- how do they operate?

Unfortunately many authors have been at great pains to emphasise the importance of the social context but have been rather less painstaking at saying what that means! Thus, my definition reflects a collection of rather disparate areas of research which have yielded important results.

Environment and social structure

Firstly I shall make a distinction between environment and the social structure.

Environment

The environment is the setting or background and has both physical and social elements. For example, one study found that experimental subjects saw the experimenter as more "status-ful" if the laboratory was untidy. Another study showed that people judged faces differently depending on whether they were in a "beautiful" or "ugly" room.[4]

Social structure

By social structure, I mean the ways in which the particular event we are looking at is organised. For example, if you attend a typical British wedding you will notice that people behave in fairly predictable ways as if they were following particular rules or codes of behaviour. You will notice that some people are behaving in very specific ways - eg the best man - as they are fulfilling specific roles. If their performance goes wrong in some way then chaos and embarrassment is likely to follow on. There is also a very definite sequence of events, eg the order of speeches at the reception. All these facts will vary depending on the location and status of the participant, eg compare a High-Society upper-class wedding with a typical church wedding or with a registry office wedding. In a different culture you will notice even more dramatic differences. But the important point I want to make here is that the participants recognise the "invisible rules of the game", ie they know what is required of them and act out their parts. People can feel very uncomfortable if they are unsure of the proceedings, and a lot of humour is based upon careful observation of the idiosyncrasies or ironies of some of our more formal occasions, eg see Robert Altman's film "A Wedding".

What are the components of the social context?

I have already distinguished between the environment and the social structure but I need to further sub-divide these categories in order to arrive at a more comprehensive definition. This is illustrated in the diagram on the next page.

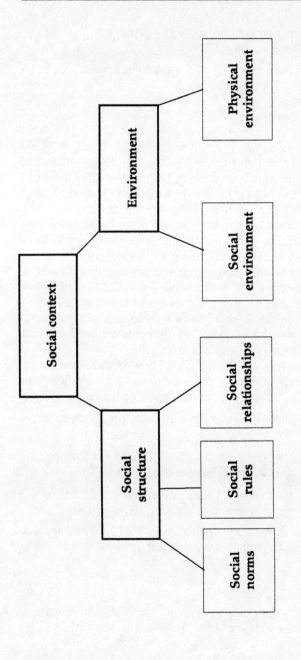

Components of the social context

I shall now discuss each of these latter categories individually.

Physical environment

The physical environment is the collection of physical objects and factors which surround us, such as the shape and size of the room, colour, lighting, heating etc. All of these can influence our behaviour in ways we might not necessarily be aware of.[5] For example, different types of neon bulb give off rather different qualities of light and it has been suggested that one type creates a more friendly atmosphere than others. At first sight this may seem a rather unlikely effect but you can easily suggest a chain of events which could lead to such a result. Harsh lighting can lead to eye strain and fatigue - this will make people feel irritable and unsettled - irritable people will tend to be short-tempered and grumpy - this will lead to arguments etc - and this will create an unfriendly atmosphere.

Consider how different physical environments influence you in terns of your mood feelings. And consider how designers try to create a particular atmosphere in buildings:

- the fast food restaurant with "bright, cheerful" colour scheme, and fast "cheerful" music

- the "posh" restaurant with subdued lighting and very soft background music

- the dentist's waiting room set out like a front room so that you "forget" where you really are!

The physical environment can affect us in a number of different ways which influence our behaviour and communication:

Direct physical effects

The environment can have direct physiological effects. If specific neon bulbs, or specific levels of heating do have predictable consequences upon us, then this could be because these have direct effects on our physiology.

Symbolic meaning

The environment can have symbolic meaning. Manufacturers of products are often very concerned about the colour of packaging because of the way certain colours have certain associations or symbolic meanings. White and blue seem to be associated with cleanliness whereas red and yellow have associations of warmth and excitement. Green is becoming a more widespread colour because of its connotations of "environment-friendliness". There is no direct physical effect here - red light is no more "exciting" to our nerve cells than white light, but we respond to them differently because of their symbolic meaning. Thus, the colour of decorations, or the feel of different furniture materials can have significant effects on how we feel and how we decide to behave.

Impact on behaviour

The physical environment can make certain behaviours easier or more difficult.

In both the UK and the USA, high-rise flats were once regarded as the answer to urban housing problems. They were relatively cheap to build and could accommodate large numbers of people. They were seen as the "modern" replacement for inner-city slums, with many advantages and no real disadvantages.

Now most high-rise flats are either problem areas or have been demolished. They have a reputation for vandalism, hooliganism, social isolation etc. Many people put up with much poorer physical home conditions rather than be moved into one. And yet these social problems were not characteristics of the housing areas they replaced where people seemed to suffer mainly from poor physical conditions, such as damp and lack of hygiene.

One major problem with high-rise flats is that they are designed in such a way as to make regular casual social meetings rather difficult. In the old properties they replaced, you usually met someone the minute you opened your front door. It was easy to have a casual chat over the back fence or on the doorstep. Local shops were at the end of the street where again you would inevitably meet neighbours and local residents. There were often very strong feelings of local community. In contrast, the high-rise developments unwittingly destroyed many of these features. And it replaced them with the worst possible compromise. Rather ironically the high-rise flat creates problems of social isolation and also lack of privacy. You are surrounded by people you have probably not met but you cannot find a place to be on your own because you are always liable to be disturbed. The partition walls are often very thin so you know exactly what TV channel next door is listening to!

Social environment

I can talk about some places which have a warm or cold physical environment because of the way they are designed and built. In the same way I can distinguish different types of social environment or social climate. Just as you might perceive another person as supportive or controlling you may also perceive a social environment as supportive or controlling or any other adjectives which suit. But one important finding is that we do seem to make consistent judgements about particular environments. And particular environments do have measurable effects. For example, a number of studies have shown that a very supportive social climate is associated with a reduction in stress or tension. And there is a good deal of research relating social factors to measurable physiological changes.[5]

One major reason why the social environment can affect our behaviour is simply that we are continually looking for information from our environment which will help us to decide what do do. Schachter[6] illustrated this point with a rather devious set of experiments where subjects were given an injection of what they thought was a vitamin with various explanations about what effect it should have. For my purposes I shall concentrate on those subjects who were not told what physical effects the "vitamin" would have. The vitamin was in fact adrenaline which has a number of predictable physiological effects - heart rate increases, etc. Each of these subjects was sitting in a waiting room thinking they were waiting for the real experiment to begin. Each thought that the other person was another waiting subject. In fact the other person was a stooge who had been instructed to act either very angrily or very elatedly. The real subjects experienced the strange physiological feelings brought on by the drug and had no explanation for them. They noticed the behaviour of the stooge and, without being consciously aware of it, they interpreted their own feelings in the same way. For example, the subjects who had been left with an "angry" stooge reported feelings of anger and hostility. Thus, these subjects were subconsciously influenced by their social environment both to feel and act in a specific way.

Social norms

In most social situations, we have a fairly clear idea of how others expect us to behave - in other words, social norms are in operation. And this demonstrates the most important feature of group norms - that a norm acts as a guide on how to behave. If you obey the norms then you are likely to be accepted by others in the situation and your behaviour will be seen as normal. If you break the norms then you may run the risk of being rejected by others and your behaviour will be seen as "odd" or even hostile. Exactly what will happen if you break a norm will depend upon a whole variety of circumstances. I shall outline a few of these later but first I shall describe a few examples of norms to make the concept clearer:

The fair day's work

One of the earliest studies on a real workgroup found that members of the group had a very clear idea of what counted as a "fair day's work for a day's pay".[7] Each member of the group consistently produced 6,000 units per day even if he could have earned more by producing more. Management continually tried to persuade the men to produce more but this was ignored. The group were suspicious of management as a result of previous events. They felt they would probably "lose out" in the long run if they did produce more and so they kept to the norm. If a worker did produce more than his target one day then he would adjust the folowing day's work to make sure he kept to the average.

The collective illusion

Sherif was one of the first researchers to demonstrate a group norm in an experimental setting.[8] He used the well-established visual illusion - the autokinetic phenomena.

If you sit in a completely darkened room and look at a tiny and stationary spot of light at one end of the room then that spot of light will appear to move. Different people see the spot move consistently different distances. For each individual, you can find out the average movement which they perceive. Sherif found that if you then put a group of three people in the room and asked them how far the spot moved then their three judgements would tend to converge and stabilise on a particular value. This group norm would then carry over to the situation where the three people later sat in the room individually. The group norm influenced their behaviour not only in the group but also outside the group.

This norming effect does not happen if the subjects are told about the illusion beforehand, presumably because they then have a rational explanation for their differences. As a result they do not experience any pressure to accommodate to the views of the other subjects.

From these examples, you can see that norms exist at different levels. The most important are cultural and group norms.

Cultural norms

These are norms which apply to all members of a given culture. For example, there are very powerful norms of politeness in Japanese culture which mean that it is considered very rude to say "no" to another person. If you wish to refuse something then you have to do it indirectly, perhaps by simply delaying your answer until the other person has given up! Many foreign businessmen who have failed to do business with the Japanese have complained how much time they have wasted in negotiations. They probably failed to recognise the "no" signals when they first appeared.

Group norms

These only apply to members of a specific group. For example, teenage gangs often develop strong norms for behaving and communicating. In another of Sherif's experiments (see Chapter 10) two groups of boys from virtually identical backgrounds were observed at summer camp. One group developed norms of loud, aggressive behaviour which included swearing and shouting. The other group developed contrasting norms which emphasised polite restrained behaviour and outlawed swearing.

Unfortunately, the concept of norm is not always as clearly-defined or as consistent as it could be:[9]

- many people do seem to constantly break specific norms and yet this is ignored or even accepted.

- it is very difficult to find any generalisation about how people should behave in a given situation which everybody agrees with. So this leaves the problem of deciding what level of agreement constitutes a norm - is it 70 per cent, 80 per cent, 90 per cent or what?

- there is often a discrepancy between what people say they will do in a situation and what they do actually do. What counts as the norm?

Social rules

Our social behaviour is guided not simply by group or cultural norms but also by specific rules which seem to apply in specific situations. The distinction between rules and norms is best illustrated by using the analogy of a team game, like football. The rules of football have mostly been written down in formal documents and specify such things as how many players can participate, how long the game is, how you score a goal, what counts as foul play etc. Even if every team obeys all the rules they will still probably develop different norms. For example in English league football, Wimbledon have developed a reputation for a very basic and physical "long-ball" style whereas Liverpool have developed a reputation for their short-passing "possession" game. Players in both these teams obey the same rules of the game but they also behave in very different ways as they fall in line with the team norms.

I shall illustrate this distinction between norms and rules again later in the chapter when we look at studies of our relationships.

Social relationships

Any communication between two people will be influenced by the relationship which exists between them. This relationship can be of different types which reflect different roles (eg friend, brother) and of different quality (eg close and informal as opposed to distant and formal). The relationship can also be affected by a number of important factors - cultural differences, gender differences, and social class differences. So in order to understand what is going on you need to take all these factors into account.

Social roles

I shall discuss the various components of social roles in more detail in the next chapter. Here I do need to emphasise how important this concept is.

Every social situation incorporates some definition of the roles that are expected of the participants. And these expected roles influence how and what people will communicate. Sometimes the roles will be rather vague or ambiguous and you have to "negotiate" with the other participants what role to adopt. For example, if you go to a party held by people you do not really know very well, what role will you adopt?

It is probably unwise to go thundering in as the life and soul of the party in case that violates the norms. On the other hand many a party has died the death because no one was willing to take on an active role in the proceedings.

There are other situations where the role requirements appear to be so strong that they do determine how individuals behave. One rather dramatic example of this is Zimbardo's prison experiment.[10] Zimbardo was interested in the effects of prison life on the individual and so he set up a mock prison. All the subjects were very carefully chosen after a series of psychological tests to make sure they were a representative group of intelligent middle-class youths. They were divided at random into prisoners and guards. The guards were equipped with typical American guards' uniforms and hats and were told that they were in charge. The only definite rule was a ban on the use of physical violence. To add realism, the prisoners were arrested by real local policemen and put through the usual signing-in procedure. They were given a uniform - a plain long smock - and left in the care of the guards.

Neither group was given any training or instruction in how to behave. Zimbardo and his colleagues sat back to observe but were soon forced to intervene. In his own words:[11]

> once the experiment began, we, as experimenters, had very little input into the guard-prisoner interaction. At that point, we were simply videotaping, and observing the drama unfold. We had intended it to last for two weeks, but the pathology we observed was so extreme, we ended the study after only six days. By "pathology" I mean that half the students who were prisoners had emotional breakdowns in less than five days. On the other hand, the guards behaved brutally, sadistically; the only difference among them was their frequency of brutal, sadistic, dehumanizing behaviour. But they all did it to some degree.

These astonishing results were not the product of sadistic or cruel minds. The "guards" after the experiment were themselves shocked and disgusted at the way they had behaved. And yet during the experiment they had been so caught up in the experience that they had been able to disregard their normal moral values. The roles had "won".

The experiment did have one very positive outcome - Zimbardo started to campaign for penal reform in the USA and has since been responsible for a number of worthy developments.

Relationship type and quality

The last ten years has seen a dramatic upsurge in research on personal relationships.[12] Some of this research has focussed on different qualities of relationship, eg love, friendship, acquaintance etc. One general conclusion concerns the relationship between certain types or styles of communication and certain types of relationship. For example, self-disclosure has already been mentioned as an important component in developing relationships (see Chapter 3). There have been other important lines of research which relate to themes mentioned in this book:

Skills

Research has suggested that there are a number of social skills differences which are associated with the ability to develop relationships - loneliness, for example:[13]

> Lonely and isolated people tend to be deficient in the sending of non-verbal signals, particularly signals of liking via face and voice.

Of course this does beg a very important question - what are the original causes of such deficiency? Do people become lonely simply because they lack skills, or do their skills deteriorate as a result of their experience and feelings

Rules and social knowledge

As I said in Chapter 4, being able to perform a skill depends on knowing what to do as well as having the ability to carry out the behaviour. People who find it difficult to strike up relationships may simply lack the knowledge and experience of the acceptable ways of doing it (they don't know the rules). For example, one study asked college students how they would try to get to know someone.[13] Their "plans" were then rated by independent judges on how likely they were to be successful. Students who were more socially isolated tended to produce plans which were seen as less effective. Their lack of social knowledge seemed to be one factor which contributed to their loneliness.

Cultural differences

There are some very important differences in the way different cultures regard different relationshps. There are different rules associated with the same relationship and this can have major differences in what and how the participants communicate. I talk about social rules below. To illustrate the influence of cultural background, Argyle reached the following conclusions after a study of differences between British, Italian, Hong Kong and Japanese informants:[13]

> It seems we place more emphasis on expressing emotions, giving opinions on intimate topics, affection and requests for help and advice than our Hong Kong and Japanese ounterparts, at least as far as intimate relationships are concerned. Close relationships, whether spouses, family, friends, or kin by marriage, or even by virtue of heterosexual intimacy (as in dating or cohabitation), are viewed as sources of support, and rules exist about using them as such. We ask for material help, disclose our personal problems and feelings, and ask for personal advice in our intimate relationships. And to a lesser extent, we apply similar rules to our less intimate acquaintances such as work colleagues and neighbours - and also use them as sources of social sup-

port. While the Hong Kong informants endorse very similar rules for husbands and wives, Japanese marriages are characterised by less emphasis on the overt expression of intimacy. And the same is true of other Japanese and Hong Kong intimate relationships.

Gender differences

Unfortunately social scientists have not always been very sensitive to differences between men and women. Researchers have assumed that the results from a study using male subjects can also be directly applied to females. Happily, more recent research has been much more careful in examining gender differences.[14]

A number of differences have been found between males and females in their communication and this has included areas such as nonverbal communication, use of influence and power, strategies, and conversational style.[15] And the differences also relate to perceptions and expectations:[16]

> differences between the sexes still exist. The way males and females report communicating and the way males and females are perceived by others to communicate is also different.

However interpretations and explanations of differences here must be approached with extreme caution for at least two fundamental reasons:

Stereotyping

Many discussions of male/female differences seem to rely on social stereotypes rather than direct observations. This is especially unfortunate at a time when:[17]

> traditional sex roles and stereotypes seem to be in a greater state of flux or change than has been the case for some time

We return to this issue in the next chapter where roles and stereotypes are discussed in more detail.

Methodology

Many of the often-quoted studies in this area are very limited in terms of their procedures and choice of subjects. For example, consider the "classic" study by Zimmerman and West[18] which concluded that men were responsible for 96 per cent of interruptions in conversation between men and women. This can of course be interpreted as evidence of domination and social power:

> Those with power and status talk more and interrupt more[19]

Ellis and Beattie[20] question how far we can generalise the results from this study on a number of grounds:

- the limited sample of subjects
  All were middle-class, under 35 and white.

- the limited nature of the conversations
  All were two person settings and only consisted of "everyday chit-chat".

- reporting of results
  Only the total number of interruptions were used to develop the conclusions. This implies that all the males act in much the same way and this disguises the fact that the male subjects differed dramatically in their behaviour. In fact, one of the eleven males did contribute nearly one-quarter of the interruptions.

- results from other studies
  They report a number of conflicting studies - for example, Beattie himself found no differences in the volume of interruptions in a study of mixed-sex university tutorial groups.

So Ellis and Beattie draw the conclusion that:

the question of male and female dominance in conversation through the medium of interruption is far from conclusively answered. The data are still somewhat contradictory, and the interpretation of the data still not certain.

Social class differences

Social class is one of the main sources of variation in behaviour and life style in society.

The author of this quote continues to discuss a wide range of social behaviours which vary in different social classes, covering just about every type of relationship you can mention.[21]

As with gender differences, there has been fierce debate over the extent and explanations of these differences. Particular debates which are especially important for interpersonal communication concern:

- the issue of language
  The suggestion that middle and working class people use different language codes has received particular attention for its significance in education (where of course most teachers are middle class).[22]

- cultural and sub-cultural differences
  Given that different classes live under very different material conditions, it is not surprising if these differences are reflected in their perceptions and expectations.

- perceptions and stereotypes
  Different stereotypes may well influence "cross-class" communication in ways which are discussed in the next chapter.

I have tried to refer to the role of cultural, gender, and class differences wherever possible in this book. However, these issues could fill a book on their own and do deserve more extended research.

Relating the components

Although it is useful to identify the separate components of the social context to exlain how they work, they never work in isolation in real situations. The best way of illustrating the sorts of interactions which occur is to look at practical examples, so I shall highlight one area of research which has important practical implications for all of us - the nature of social relationships.

I have already suggested that social contact is very important for human beings. I can be more specific - it is not just the quantity but also the quality of social contact which is important. There is ample evidence that the quality of relationships we have with other people can influence our health, and happiness. Good relationships affect these variables in positive ways, poor or non-existent relationships can have serious harmful effects.

One aspect of this is whether we follow the rules which others recognise as important in the particular relationship. There are some important differences here :

Generality
Rules differ in their general application For example, Argyle found that:[13]

- there are a small number of rules which can apply to all these relationships (eg respect the other person's privacy)

- there are rules which are important to some relationships but not to others (eg "Engage in joking and teasing with the other person" is an important friendship and marriage rule but is not a significant neighbour rule)

Cultural differences

Different cultures may observe different rules for the same relationship

Once again the work of Michael Argyle and colleagues can illustrate this point.[13] They distributed the same questionnaire on relationship rules to men and women in Italy, Hong Kong, Japan and Britain. Each respondent was asked their opinion on how far thirty-three rules could be applied to a range of relationships, eg husband-wife, doctor-patient. Only four of the rules were rated important in all relationships in all cultures:

- respect the other person's privacy

- look the other person in the eye during conversation

- do not discuss that which is said in confidence with the other person

- do not criticise the other person publicly

Group differences

Different groups within one society or culture will endorse rules differently.

Argyle found both sex and age differences in the endorsement of specific rules for virtually all the relationships they studied:

- there were interesting sex differences in relation to rules of intimacy. Although in many relationships women feel it is more important to express and share emotions, they also endorse rules about privacy more than men. This was true for all four cultures.

- you would probably expect to find age differences in adherence to rules, given the rate of social change which has occurred over the last 20/30 years. This role of change has also affected our relationships as current statistics and attitudes on marriage, divorce and living together will illustrate. Argyle found the greatest discrepancy between young and old subjects in the British sample. One fairly consistent difference across its culture concerned intimacy rules - younger subjects felt you should express emotions more generally.

The time factor - how relationships develop

As well as identifying how the various components of the social context can interrelate, we must not forget that these factors can change over time. Again, the study of our relationships can illustrate this point. Communication is an essential ingredient in all stages of a relationship and most investigators have suggested that any relationship is likely to pass through a series of stages. We can see different aspects of communication at each of these different stages.[23] To explain the stages, we can look at some of the factors involved in making friends.

Becoming aware of others

Before you can establish a relationship with someone you obviously need to be aware of their existence. And you need to have developed an impression of them. Factors which I have already discussed under the heading of Social Perception are also relevant here. Particularly important are the influence of physical proximity, social similarity and physical attractiveness. If we are placed in close physical proximity with other people, as in the corridor of a student hall of residence or a work group in a department, then we are likely to develop friendships within that group of people. We are also likely to notice others who seem to come from similar social backgrounds, and we shall be looking for verbal and non-verbal codes such as dress, mannerisms, accent etc. Physical attractiveness is a further powerful influence. Of course, you may not judge physical attractiveness in the way that I do, but we may be strongly influenced by stereotypes. Psychologists have found that there is a clear and positive stereotype of "physically attractive persons" which gives them a number of advantages over us lesser mortals - for example, they are usually seen as more competent and more intelligent.[23]

Making contact

You are in your first morning of a new job. Your boss introduces you to a person who will be one of your main team members. You go to the coffee machine with him or her. What do you talk about? How do you get the relationship off to a good start?

First meetings like this are likely to have a fairly predictable pattern of communication with the following characteristics:

- people exchange non-controversial information about themselves

- they talk about their background and tend to stick to facts rather than opinions

- the initial few minutes will involve fairly rapid turn-taking using question-answer sequences

This pattern is not very surprising: exchanging background information is a fairly interesting way of passing time and is not likely to lead to any conflict. More importantly it allows each person to gather information which will enable them to decide whether to develop the relationship. If I find from this initial encounter that you have a similar background to me then I may well decide to try to develop a close relationship. Or I may decide that you are a bit "wet" , perhaps because you seem to live up to one of my negative stereotypes.

There's a couple of other interesting points about these initial exchanges:

- if one person in the conversation does not follow the typical pattern then confusion or conflict will develop

100

- we can be heavily influenced by stereotypes (and gender/sex stereotypes may be especially important as discussed in the next chapter)

- the context may well mean that we can safely assume that the other person has certain attitudes.
  If I happen to meet you dressed in your famous Captain Kirk disguise wearing your Spock ears in the lobby of a hotel where a trekkies convention is being held, then I can start the conversation on a rather different basis than if we met in the same attire in a dentists' waiting room.

Developing contact into friendship

This is the next stage in developing a relationship. There are a number of interesting aspects to this process:

- we need to self-disclose to each other so that we can deepen our understanding of each other. If I self-disclose to you then I will expect you to reciprocate. In fact you will probably feel obligated to respond. And I can use this to push the relationship along. If you do not want to push the relationship along at the same pace, you will have to "slow me down".

- we can use particular strategies to express our commitment to the other person, eg we develop mutual trust when I trust you with some information which I see as private and vice versa

- we need to adapt to each others' styles of communication

- both verbal and nonverbal cues are important

- we need to act in a way which is appropriate to the level of relationship we have reached

101

- we need to achieve "balance".
  In order to make the relationship mutually satisfying, we need to agree on what each of us is
  going to "put in" to the relationship. This is
  probably never consciously discussed but problems will soon emerge if one of us feels the
  other is not "playing fair".

Conclusion

Perhaps the most important conclusion to emerge from this
chapter is simply to re-affirm the importance of the social
context. However, it is also important to try to consider the
social context in more detail and identify the components
which are influencing particular examples of communication. For example, several important principles were identified in the last discussion of how friendships develop. These
principles are not absolute and will vary depending upon
context. What is considered to be "fair" or "balanced" will
depend upon a range of social rules, norms and perceptions.
And this highlights my final point - the factors identified in
this chapter are interdependent and so their impact in any
given situation may well be the result of quite a complicated
process.

Notes

1 See the quote from McQuail on page 2 of Chapter 1.

2 There is a growing interest in problems of communication between cultures. For example :

   W. B. Gudykunst and Y.Y. Kim (1992) *Communicating with Strangers*, 2nd edn, McGraw-Hill

3 There is a very extensive literature which debates the problems of explaining human behaviour. If you want to explore the issues surrounding psychological approaches, a good starter is the following :

   G. Westland (1978) *Current Crises of Psychology*, Heinemann

4 Both of these examples are taken from an article by Canter et al., reprinted in:

   A. Furnham and M. Argyle, eds (1981) *The Psychology of Social Situations*, Pergamon

5 For an interesting analysis of environmental effects, see Chapter 10 of:

   M. Argyle, A. Furnham, and E. J. A. Graham (1981) *Social Situations*, Cambridge University Press

6 This very famous experiment is summarised in most social psychology textbooks. You will find a very detailed analysis of its results in:

   P. Ashworth (1979) *Social Interaction and Consciousness*, John Wiley

7 This example is taken from the Bank Wiring Observation Room study which was part of the Hawthorne studies, one of the first systematic studies of social groups. For further details see:

   J. A. C. Brown (1964) *The Social Psychology of Industry*, Penguin

M. S. Olmsted and A. P. Hare (1978) *The Small Group*, 2nd edn, Random House

8   For a useful discussion of group norms, along with more detail of Sherif's work, see :

G. Gaskell and P. Sealy (1976) *Groups - Coursebook for D305 Block 13*, Open University Press

9   Peter Smith discusses this problem and describes a classroom exercise to illustrate it in Chapter 15 of:

G. M. Breakwell, H. Foot and R. Gilmour (1989) *Doing Social Psychology: Laboratory and Field Exercises*, 2nd edn, Cambridge University Press/British Psychological Society. First edition published in 1982 as *Social Psychology : A Practical Manual*, Macmillan

10 A useful description of this experiment can be found in:

B. H. Raven and J. Z. Rubin (1983) *Social Psychology*, 2nd edn, Wiley

11 This quote is taken from a lengthy discussion with Zimbardo in :

R. I. Evans (1980) *The Making of Social Psychology: Discussions with Creative Contributors*, Wiley

12 For example, consult the five volumes in Steve Duck's major series, or see his recently revised basic text in this area:

S. Duck and R. Gilmour (1981-5) *Personal Relationships*, vols 1-5, Academic Press

S. Duck (1992) *Human Relationships*, 2nd edn, Sage

13 For the studies quoted in this chapter and a general summary of recent research in this area, see:

M. Argyle and M. Henderson (1985) *The Anatomy of Friendships*, Penguin

14 See the chapter on sex roles and sex differences (Chapter 12) in Raven and Rubin (see 10 above).

15 For a much fuller list of areas and the associated references, see B. H. Spitzberg and C. C. Brunner's chapter in:

C. M. Lont and S. A. Friedley , eds (1989) *Beyond Boundaries: Sex and Gender Diversity in Communication*, George Mason University Press

16 See the chapter by Brenda Pruett on communicator style differences in Lont and Friedley.

17 See the chapter on sex roles and work by Oonagh Hartnett and Jenny Bradley in:

D. J. Hargreaves and A. M. Colley, eds (1986) *The Psychology of Sex Roles*, Harper and Row

18 This study is described in Zimmerman and West's chapter in:

B. Thorpe and N. Henley, eds (1975) *Language and Sex: Difference and Dominance*, Newbury House

19 This quote is taken from a newspaper article where Dale Spender raises many of these arguments - "Don't keep your trap shut" *Guardian*, August 23, 1982. For more detailed treatment, see:

D. Spender (1982) *Manmade Language*, Routledge and Kegan Paul

20 See p 103ff in:

A. Ellis and G. Beattie (1986) *The Psychology of Language and Communication*, Weidenfeld and Nicholson

21 The quote comes from Chapter 8 of the text by Argyle. The book by Tom Bottomore provides an overview of the complexities of social class from a sociological perspective:

M. Argyle (1992) *The Social Psychology of Everyday Life*, Routledge

T. Bottomore (1991) *Classes in Modern Society*, 2nd edn, Harper Collins

22 This view was developed in the UK by Basil Bernstein. For an accessible discussion of his work, see:

M. Montgomery (1987) *An Introduction to Language and Society*, Methuen

23 Steve Duck has been a major researcher in these areas - see note 12 above - and he also provides a very good introduction to the study of relationships and theories of stages in:

S. Duck (1988) *Relating to Others*, Open University Press

6

Social identity

In this chapter, I shall :

- identify the main components of our social identity
- explain how these components influence the way we communicate with other people

What is social identity?

Perhaps the best way of showing what I mean by social identity is by using an example. I have already discussed the conversation between Dr Poussaint and the policeman. If we look again at this in a little more detail and concentrate on Dr Poussaint, we can notice the various components of social identity at work.

Dr Poussaint was not a very aggressive or outspoken person. His colleagues and friends would describe his **personality** as polite, gentle and considerate. This was the way he usually behaved to other people and was not usually greeted in a hostile way. So he was taken aback when he was attacked in such a way. He was not used to this treatment.

Dr Poussaint saw himself as respectable and law-abiding. He was proud of his status in the community and worked hard to maintain it. The policeman's behaviour had such an effect because of the picture which Dr Poussaint had of himself, his **self-concept**.

Dr Poussaint was a qualified medical doctor. He was very aware that he was expected to behave in certain ways because of the **role** he occupied. This role also meant that he was usually accorded a fair degree of respect by other people. The policeman's attack deliberately broke the usual rules!

This example suggests that there are three components of social identity - personality, self-concept, and role.[1] In most situations, these are strongly related to another. For example, if you have a very outgoing personality then you will probably see yourself as socially confident and likeable and you will take on roles which complement this view of yourself, eg party organiser. This does not mean that our behaviour is totally or even primarily determined by our personality (I shall discuss this in more detail later). There is ample evidence which suggests that if people are thrust into particular roles then this can affect both their self-concept and their personality. I shall look at some of these processes in more detail by examining each component in them.

Personality

Most definitions of human personality reflect a number of general principles that seem to be born out in everyday life:[2]

- each of us has a specific set of personal characteristics
- this set of characteristics is fairly stable over time
- these characteristics influence how we behave and communicate

In recent years, however, some psychologists have adopted a rather different perspective on human personality. They have decided that our personalities are not such a powerful influence on our behaviour after all. There have been several factors which have contributed to this change of mind:

The search for adequate theory

There are several psychological theories of human personality. There is no one theory which is universally accepted. All of the theories proposed so far seem to have important limitations.

Problems of measurement and prediction

Personality tests or measures do not seem to be very good at predicting how people actually will behave. There are several problems here:

Personality types

Many theories try to categorise people into types and then investigate the properties of each type. You have probably heard of the distinction between extrovert and introvert personalities. Researchers have suggested a number of significant differences between the true extravert and the introvert:

- extroverts can be described as "tough-minded individuals who need strong and varied exter-

nal stimulation".[3]
They are sociable, optimistic, impulsive etc.

- introverts are "tender-minded people who experience strong emotions and who do not need the extrovert's intensity of external stimuli". They are quiet, introspective, pessimistic etc.

Unfortunately for the researchers relatively few of us are "full" types. Most of us possess a mixture of extravert and introvert characteristics, which makes predicting our behaviour more uncertain.

Consistency of behaviour

When you examine closely how people actually behave in different situations, you find that they are often not very "consistent". A person who is usually quite quiet and shy may behave in a very extrovert manner in some situations.

As a result of these factors psychologists have focussed attention upon the interaction between individual personalities and the situations they find themselves in. I shall return to the influence of situations in Chapter 7.

My own view of human personality follows these developments:

- we do possess a range of personal character traits

- these traits do influence how we behave and communicate

- these traits are *only one* influence upon our behaviour

Following this line of argument, I suggest that your personality influences your communication in two main ways:

Predispositions

Our personality characteristics predispose us to behave in certain ways.

Limitations

Our personality characteristics establish very broad limits for our communication. This is like the way physical characteristics can limit what you do physically. For example, it is very difficult to be a good long-distance runner unless you have a particular sort of physique. Similarly with psychological characteristics, our personality establishes certain limitations. Of course, these are not absolute limitations - if you are aware of your limitations you may be able to devise strategies to overcome them. Consider the case of the person who would wish to become a great stage comedian but who is hampered with problems - he can't remember jokes and his sense of timing is rotten. On the one hand, we could perhaps overcome his limitations by determined training. Who knows what ten years at the Les Dawson Charm School could do for him? On the other hand, he could play on his "weaknesses" and develop an act based upon his "incompetence", perhaps borrowing from classic acts like Tommy Cooper.

To return to more serious issues, someone who scores very high or low on a particular personality scale such as intoversion/extraversion may have real psychological problems in coping with everyday life. But an extreme may be an "ambiguous gift".[3] Individuals who are aware of their own tendencies may be able to control them and use them to advantage. And this raises the question of self-awareness which is at the heart of any discussion of the self-concept.

Self-concept

One of the distinctive features of human beings as a species is that we can think about our own actions and reactions. Of course, we take this ability for granted. But consider the range of things it enables us to do. It allows us to reflect upon our past experiences and make plans for the future. It enables us to develop ideas about ourselves. It means that we can also develop opinions about how other people see us. And how we would like to be seen by other people.

This then is the essential idea behind the self-concept. The self-concept has been defined by Carl Rogers as an:[4]

> organised, fluid, but consistent conceptual pattern
> of perceptions of characteristics and relationships of
> the "I" or the "me" , together with values attached to
> these concepts

Rogers makes the distinction between "I" and "me". This distinction was elaborated by George Herbert Mead as a way of representing how human beings come to develop a concept of themselves.[5] The "I" represents the self as actor and the "me" represents the self's reflections about itself. This may be clearer with some examples of how these ideas develop.

The "I"

Very young babies do not seem to distinguish between their own bodies and their surroundings. They do not have a clear idea of themselves as actors who can control objects around them. For example, when a rattle is dropped out of view babies seem to believe it has disappeared and no longer exists. As they become older they realise that they can act independently of their surroundings and go looking for the rattle. As they become older still, they actively seek to become independent. Witness the determination with which young children attempt to do basic jobs like putting clothes on. The adult who attempts to intervene can receive a very hostile response even when the child is stuggling against all odds. For example, Markova refers to some classic research film of young children which shows: [6]

> children's tremendous persistence...in trying to sit
> on a stone without realising that one must turn one's
> back to the stone if one wants to sit on it

So these children have developed the "I", what Markova refers to as - "the spontaneous and acting component of the self".

The "me"

The "me" has been described as the "reflective and evaluative" component of the self. In order to evaluate your own actions you need to be able to consider them "from outside" - in other words you must be able to observe your own behaviour as if you were another person. You must be able to understand how other people might react to your actions and understand their thoughts and feelings.

The self-concept as personal theory

Another way of understanding the self-concept is to see it as a theory which the individual uses in everyday life. It is a theory that the individual has constructed about him or herself, sometimes consciously but sometimes unwittingly. And it is part of a broader theory which the individual holds with respect to their entire range of significant experience.

Like theories used by scientists, the self theory is a conceptual tool for accomplishing a purpose. Two basic functions, which are important for my analysis are:

Self-esteem
Self-esteem is an individual's estimation of their worth or value. Although we all seem to have a very basic motivation to develop positive self-esteem there is plenty of evidence that many people do not achieve this - they develop low self-esteem and life can become a very miserable and dispiriting experience.

Organising information
The self-concept helps us to organise the data of experience in a manner that can be coped with effectively. We are surrounded by so much information which we could attend to about our activities in the world that we would be

swamped if we tried to deal with all of it. We need to simplify the information and the self-concept acts as an organising principle so we can think constructively about ourselves without considering all the details of all our actions all of the time.

This proposition that the self-concept is a theory has much in common with an influential view[7] that the individual, going about the business of attempting to solve the problems of everyday living, proceeds in a manner similar to that of the scientist who is attempting to solve more impersonal problems:

both continuously make and test hypotheses

The scientist may develop a hypothesis about certain chemicals - the influence of PCFC on the ozone layer - and make observations and/or develop experiments to see if the hypothesis is valid. In the same way we develop hypotheses about the world around us and test them out. As I was huddled over word-processor battling with the first draft of this chapter, my younger son (5 years old at the time) popped in to see me to reveal that he "cannot go to sleep because the dogs are barking and could he go to sleep in the bedroom on the other side of the house". This is his latest and most creative variant on his regular bed-time theme of wanting to stay up a bit longer. He is checking me out to see if this story is any more successful than last night's version of "I'm not all that sleepy". After a few minutes of amiable conversation where I assure him that "the dogs will go to sleep themselves in a minute", he trots back to bed to reflect on the success of tonight's creativity. Like all children, he is continually generating ideas of new social behaviours and trying them out to see if they work. Adults also do this of course, although perhaps not so creatively.

both scientists and ordinary individuals revise their concepts accordingly

If the scientific experiment does not work then the scientist develops a new hypothesis - a different way of explaining events. If my social actions do not work then I also have to revise my social concepts and perhaps become more sophisticated in my assessment of which actions will achieve the desired effect. As I finished typing this last sentence on the word-processor in the upstairs spare room, our phone rang in the kitchen. By the time I had got downstairs my younger son had answered the phone - "I heard it ringing and I thought I'd better answer it!". His early action of complaining about the dogs had earned a short "stay of bed-time". But a helpful action is another very useful strategy for postponing the possibility of having to go to sleep. Although he is generally very good at answering the phone I cannot help noticing that he is not usually as quick during the hours of play!

both organise their observations into "schemata" which then are organised into a network of broader schemata called theories

The scientist takes a number of observations and extracts more fundamental principles. These principles are then developed into systematic theories which apply within certain limits. An apple falling on the head, along with many other observations and tests, can be developed into the theory of gravity. Likewise we may have observed how our parents behave towards us and, consciously or sub-consciously, developed our ideas of what acting like a parent involves. As a result we develop ways of reacting to our parents and we develop ideas of how we are going to behave when we become parents. If we sit down and think about it we can probably express what these theories contain - almost certainly they will include principles of reward and punishment, and concepts of discipline, responsibility and personal freedom.

If our experience were not so arranged then it would be impossible to behave effectively in a complex world with innumerable conflicting demands. Further, without such a system the individual would be overwhelmed by innumerable isolated details that would have to be recalled to guide any particular piece of behaviour.

There is one important difference between my approach and Kelly's - Kelly assigns little significance to emotion and his methods concentrate on thoughts and cognitions. I believe we must give emotion a position of central importance in discussing the self-concept. More on this later.

But how does the self-concept develop?

Mead proposed that the self-concept arises in social inter-action as an outgrowth of the individual's concern about how others react to him. In order to anticipate other people's reactions so that s/he can behave accordingly, the individual learns to perceive the world as these other people do. By incorporating estimates of how the "generalised other" would respond to certain actions, the individual acquires a source of internal regulation. This serves to guide and stabilise behaviour in the absence of external pressures.

Other social scientists have emphasised the interaction of the child with significant others, particularly the mother figure, rather than with society at large.

The role of communication

At this point we can emphasise the role of communication in developing the self-concept. Take the example of our knowledge of our own bodies, eg tall versus short. Both of these descriptions are obviously relative terms - taller/shorter than what? - but they have general connotations in our society. The "hero" in fiction is usually represented as tall whereas comic characters are often represented as short people, so much so that at least one of the classic film stars of Hollywood, Alan Ladd, had to resort to tricks like standing on a box and being filmed from specific angles so as not to reveal to the watching millions that he was smaller than most of his leading ladies.

So how do people acquire this item of self-description? There are two main ways

- direct training - we're actually told directly

- indirect training - we infer it from a variety of cues which are capable of indicating that we have characteristics in common with some people, yet different from others. Children are usually fascinated by the discovery that they have hands and feet that look more like other people's than like those of the dog or cat that inhabit the same household.
In the same way we learn that people differ in behavioural characteristics, such as friendliness, aggressiveness, and helpfulness.

Both these methods rely on communication, and one important implication of this approach is the degree by which we can be affected by other people's impressions of us. This is why many psychologists have stressed the importance of the communications we receive from our parents or parent-figures in developing our early ideas of ourselves.

For example, some researchers distinguish three types of response we can make to each other in any interaction: confirmation, rejection, or disconfirmation.[8] These have very different implications for the self-concept of the person being communicated to.

Confirmation
If I confirm you then I take account of what you say, I pay attention to you and I accept you have the right to express whatever you are saying.

Rejection
If I reject you then I do not accept what you say but I do implicitly accept that you have the right to express yourself in that way.

Disconfirmation
If I disconfirm you then not only do I reject what you say but I also reject your very presence as a person. I may ignore you, or treat what you say as irrelevant, or even deliberately misinterpret it.

Both confirmation and rejection implicitly recognise the other person's self-concept as valid. Disconfirmation threatens this validity. For a very simple example, take this mother-child interchange:[9]

"Look, mom, I found a snail."

"Go wash your hands."

The mother ignores the content of the boy's speech and delivers a very definite judgement of irrelevance which was probably reinforced by accompanying nonverbal signals of distaste. This one incident may not be deeply significant. But what if the process is repeated time and time again? And what if it occurs when the child is trying to say something which he/she considers important.

For a more fundamental example consider the anecdote from a well-known female author.[10] As a child she felt her father had continually picked on her and dismissed her achievements. When she published her first novel and brought a copy home, her father greeted her with a very powerful disconfirming message. He looked at the book and commented:

"Cost £4.95 .. is it really worth it?"

One consequence of continual disconfirmation could be the development of low self-esteem. And of course your level of self-esteem is reflected in your communication. A high degree of self-esteem is likely to lead to a confident, assertive communication style; a low degree to a tentative pessimistic style.

Social roles

The term "role" originally came from the theatre. We talk about the various roles which the actors play when they give a performance. Some social scientists have been keen to develop this as an analogy with social life in general.[11] The

118

notion is that we spend a good deal of everyday life "performing", ie we play parts which are largely predetermined.

I shall return to this analogy later but first I need to spell out the concept of role in more detail.

It was Ralph Linton, an American sociologist, who first popularised the concept of role in social science.[12] He was trying to develop a set of concepts which explained how human society was organised. He concluded that every society contained a variety of positions. For each position there was a status, which gave your place in the pecking order of society, and a role, which prescribed the expected behaviour and attitudes.

People knew how to behave because of these roles. If you took up a position in society you would know how to behave because you knew what the role involved. This of course also means that you know how and what to communicate. Understanding society was a matter of outlining the roles for every position in that society.

This approach became very influential but some problems became apparent. It offers a rather "static" view of society whereas we know that society does change over time. Roles do change. Also we can see that people do not necessarily agree on what a specific role involves. For example, there has recently been a lot of argument over the role of clergyman:

- should they be involved in political debates?

- should women be allowed to occupy the role?

There are a number of ways of dealing with these questions. All of them have implications for communication.

Role Set

No social role exists in isolation. Any given role is always related to other roles. You can hardly be a teacher unless there are pupils or students. In fact, for every given role (usually called the focal role), there are a number of other roles which are related to it. These other roles are called the role set. The most important thing about these roles in the

119

role set is that each one makes demands upon the focal role. These demands are usually called the sent role. A diagram and an example should make this clearer.

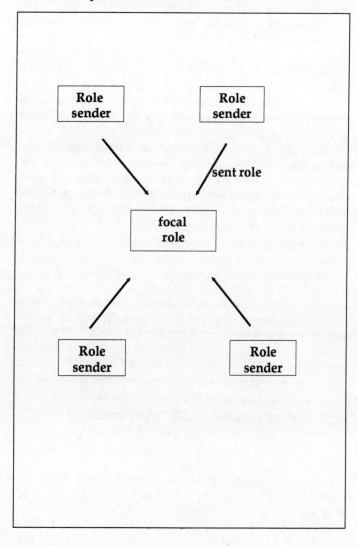

Take the example of students as a focal role. Any student is likely to know her own ideas on how to behave as a student. She will find that other people in other roles expect her to behave in particular ways, ie they act as "role senders". This gives rise to another phenomenon which has very important implications for communication -

Role conflict

Role conflict occurs when there is some discrepancy between these different expectations. There are several varieties of role conflict. Perhaps the most significant is what is referred to as "conflict-between-role-senders". Going back to my student example, she may find that lecturers expect her to devote virtually all her spare time to studying; other students may expect her to participate fully in union social activities. There will be other possibly conflicting pressures from other role senders - family, friends etc - which she has to reconcile.

Role obligations

If different occupants of the same role seem to behave rather differently, perhaps this is because they have a slightly different idea of their role obligations. Any role is liable to have a wider range of obligations associated with it. To make things even more complicated, there are likely to be different types or levels of obligation. Dahrendorf talks of three levels of obligations associated with any given role:[13]

- MUST DO
  These are activities which role occupants must do. If they do not, they will feel definite sanctions, probably legal ones.

- SHOULD DO
  These are activities which role occupants should do but where the prospect of sanctions is not so strong if they fail.

- CAN DO

  These are activities which are not "required" but which the effective role-player often includes.

Negotiated roles

Another approach which has emerged stresses that social roles are not totally laid down or predetermined.[14] To return to the theatre analogy: in most plays, all the lines and stage directions are usually written down for the actors. However, the directors and actors can make an enormous difference to the play depending upon how they interpret the roles. They obviously know how to work together and have to plan how their roles will relate to one another. In other words they have to negotiate roles with one another.

These processes of interpretation and negotiation also occur in everyday social life. For example, take a role which is fraught with problems - the role of parent. There are a number of ways in which husbands and wives can interpret their respective roles.

Apart from the thorny question of what each partner should do, they have to negotiate how they do it and who does what. Problems arise when this negotiation does not take place. This does not mean that every married couple necessarily sit down and discuss how they relate to one another, in the way that actors and directors discuss plays. Usually this negotiation in everyday life is a matter of gradual accommodation and change.

Another implication of this approach is the suggestion that all successful social interaction and communication depends upon the respective participants adopting complementary roles. This has been highlighted in recent studies of how people cope in embarrassing situations.

Conclusion

When we behave we decide upon our actions in terms of how those actions relate to the various components of our social identity. Of course, we do not necessarily do this consciously - many of our decisions are taken subconsciously. It is probably only when we experience conflict such as role conflict that we become aware of some of these processes. Perhaps we should think about these processes more often as misunderstanding and conflict frequently arise from behaviour based on different interpretations of our social identity.

Notes

1 This account of personality theory is very brief and se-
lective, as you will see if you refer to any good general
textbook in the area, such as Pervin. For an alternative
and perhaps more controversial account which tries
to chart the differences and similarities between different approaches, see Cook:

L. A. Pervin (1990) *Handbook of Personality*, Guilford
Press

M. Cook (1984) *Levels of Personality*, Holt Rinehart
Winston

2 For an accessible introduction to this area which also
looks at practical applications of personality testing,
see Chapter 6 of:

A. Huczynski and D. Buchanan (1991) *Organisational
Behaviour*, 2nd edn, Prentice Hall

3 The quotes are taken from Huczynski and Buchanan's
account of the work of Hans Eysenck , who has developed one of the most sophisticated theories related
to these personality types. For a practical "do-it-your-
self" demonstration, see:

H. J. Eysenck and G. Wilson (1975) *Know Your Own
Personality*, Maurice Temple Smith

4 Carl Rogers developed this theory as part of an
approach to psychotherapy, described in Chapter 10
of his 1951 book. See his later work for examples of
the applications of these ideas:

C. Rogers (1951) *Client-centred Therapy: Its Current
Practice, Implications and Theory*, Houghton Mifflin

C. Rogers (1961) *On Becoming a Person*, Houghton
Mifflin

C. Rogers and B. Stevens (1973) *Person to Person*,
Houghton Mifflin

5   Mead's ideas became enormously influential in sociology/social psychology, although they were not published till after his death:

G. H. Mead (1934) *Mind, Self and Society*, University of Chicago

6   Markova gives a very rich account of how we develop our self-awareness and how this depends upon communication in:

I. Markova (1987) *Human Awareness*, Hutchinson

7   This view was first proposed by George Kelly and then developed by researchers working with personal construct theory - see Chapter 7.

8   See:

P. Watzlawick, J. Beavin and D. D. Jackson (1967) *Pragmatics and Human Communication*, Norton

9   This example comes from Ruesch. The book by Ruesch and Bateson was very influential in highlighting the possible impact of these forms of communication:

J. Ruesch (1957) *Disturbed Communication*, Norton

J. Ruesch and G. Bateson (1968) *Communication: The Social Matrix of Psychiatry*, Norton

10   I overheard this in a BBC Radio 2 interview by Anne Robinson. Unfortunately I was listening in the car and was unable to catch any more details!

11   Erving Goffman is the most famous exponent of this perspective. For example, see:

E. Goffman (1969) *The Presentation of Self in Everyday Life*, Penguin

12   Linton originally published his ideas in the 1920s. Analysis of social roles became a central concern for

sociologists. For an organisational application of this approach, see Chapter 3 of the book by Handy:

C. B. Handy (1981) *Understanding Organisations*, 2nd edn, Penguin

13 Dahrendorf enlarges upon these distinctions in:

R. Dahrendorf (1973) *Homo Sociologicus*, Routledge and Kegan Paul

7

Social perception

In this chapter, I shall:

- define and illustrate the importance of social perception
- explain and examine a number of theoretical approaches which have been used to explain social perception
- discuss some important categories of information which we perceive and interpret in social events
- examine issues of accuracy and bias in social perceptions

What is social perception?

By social perception, I mean those processes whereby an individual makes sense of and interprets the nature of the other people involved in the conversation, and the nature of the setting in which they find themselves. If that sounds rather a mouthful then I can easily illustrate the importance of social perception with a few examples:

The new lecturer example

In one very famous experiment, Harold Kelley provided a group of university students with a short written description of a visiting lecturer just before he lectured to them for the first time.[1] Unbeknown to the students, two forms of the description were distributed at random. The only difference between the two forms was that the phrase "very warm" was used to describe the lecturer on one version, and the phrase "rather cold" was used on the other. So each student read a description of Mr X like this:

> Mr X is a graduate student in the Department of Economics and Social Science here at M.I.T. He has had three semesters of teaching experience in psychology at another college. This is his first semester teaching Ec.70. He is 26 years old, a veteran, and married. People who know him consider him to be a rather cold (or, "very warm") person, industrious, critical, practical, and determined.

After the class (which included a discussion session lasting about 20 minutes), Kelley asked the students to rate the lecturer. There were marked differences in these ratings depending on which prior description the student had read. "Warm" students saw the lecturer as successful, popular, happy, humorous etc. "Cold" students saw the lecturer as stingy, unsuccessful, unpopular and unhappy. There was also a marked difference in class participation. Fifty-six per cent of the "warm" students took part in the discussion; only 32 per cent of the "cold" students did so.

This experiment suggests that there is some truth in the statement that we see what we expect to see. The students gained their initial impression from the written description and seemed to stick to it regardless of the evidence available to them. They also *behaved* in accordance with what they thought was true rather than actual events. This behaviour then reinforced their initial impression. If you participate in a discussion then you're liable to see the leader more positively than if you sit aloof simply because you've received some reactions from him.

This is an example of a "self-fulfilling prophecy" - someone is "labelled" in a particular way; this makes other people expect that person to behave in specific ways; these other people then behave to the labelled person on the basis of their expectations; the person reacts and probably lives up to the expectations.[2] An example may make this clearer. Suppose a new pupil arrives at a school after a rumour that he is a "trouble-maker". The other pupils and teachers will expect him to live up to this reputation and may well greet him in a suspicious or hostile way. The newcomer reacts to what he see as a hostile welcome, possibly by retaliating in a hostile way, and the "prophecy" has come true. Of course, labels can also be positive but the process will be the same.

There is some evidence that self-fulfilling prophecies can have long-term effects. Unfortunately Kelley's experiment only looked at a fairly short event. The class only lasted twenty minutes. What would have happened to the students' perceptions if the class had lasted longer, or if they had seen the lecturer again on a number of occasions?

The spectators' example

Another classic experiment within social psychology studied the perceptions of spectators after a particularly rough game of American football between Dartmouth and Princeton.[1] The investigators asked spectators who was responsible for the rough play. If you have ever been involved in team sports you will probably not be surprised to learn that the supporters' perceptions were consistently different. For example, only 36 per cent of the Dartmouth students thought that their team had started the rough play whereas 86 per cent of the Princeton students thought that the Dartmouth team had.

The social constructs example

I have already referred to Forgas' study[3] where he examined the different perceptions of Oxford students and housewives. As well as having rather different sets of social constructs these two groups interpreted similar situations very differently. For example, Forgas found that the two groups had very different reactions to "socialising with friends":

> Students seem to regard episodes involving entertainments and socialising with friends with great self-confidence. The very different subjective definition of these interactions, involving nearly indistinguishable activities and objective characteristics, suggests that a classification of episodes in terms of objective factors may not tap the psychologically meaningful differences. While "socialising with friends" for students is a natural, self-selected entertainment, for housewives it may be a more formal, organised affair, with an element of self-presentation and potential loss of face.

These differences reflect differences in the way the different groups see the situation. They do not represent systematic differences in personality characteristics. For example, the results do not simply mean that the students surveyed were all supremely self-confident. In fact they reported frequent feelings of lacking self-confidence in other situations, eg situations where you have to become acquainted with strangers, such as parties.

In explaining these differences in perception we must also pay attention to the social context. For example the housewives group came from middle-class areas and so were influenced by middle-class norms.

How can we explain social perception?

There has now been considerable research on the ways in which we perceive other people. Unfortunately there has been much less attention paid to our perception of social situations. So I shall concentrate on the evidence that concerns person perception.

Person perception

The early work on person perception tended to focus on how people interpreted various personality traits.[4] Researchers looked at which traits seemed to be most important and which traits seemed to go together. Some interesting conclusions came from this work which was based on the notion of implicit personality theory, ie that we all have organised ideas of what personality traits usually go together. More recent developments have concentrated on how people develop their own ideas about other people (attribution theory) and on how these ideas are organised (personal construct theory). Unfortunately, all these researches developed from rather different backgrounds and so it is difficult to integrate them very smoothly into one explanation. However, I shall make some suggestions on this once I have examined each in turn.

Implicit personality theory

This notion is based upon a number of important findings:

Coherent perceptions
People do have a coherent picture of which personality traits tend to go together in other people. For example if you hear someone described as warm then you are also liable to think that person is popular, happy, successful etc. Some of these

associations seem to be very strong whereas others are relatively weak. For example, if you ask people to judge the intelligence of others based on a selection of photographs, then they will tend to choose people wearing glasses as more intelligent than those without. This also applies when you ask for first impressions of people who have only just met. However, after only a few minutes of conversation the effect disappears. There is no longer any consistent difference associated with wearing glasses. People are obviously using other cues from the conversation.

Organised perceptions

These impressions are organised so that some traits are much more important or central than others. For example, I have already described Kelley's "warm/cold" experiment. These traits - warm and cold - do seem to be very influential. In a set of earlier experiments,[7] Asch provided students with a list of seven traits which were characteristic of individual X. The students then had to write a general description of X and also judge him on various dimensions. If X was described as warm or cold these adjectives coloured the whole descriptions which emerged along the lines that Kelley also found. Substituting other terms such as polite or blunt for warm or cold made much less of a difference.

Although this approach generated a great deal of interesting research it did not provide very convincing answers to a number of important questions, in particular:

- how are various traits organised?
- why are certain traits central?

There has been more recent research designed to answer these questions but the general focus has moved on to the question of how people arrive at their own often very unique views on other people.

Personal construct theory

This theory was first developed by George Kelly who was concerned that theories such as implicit personality theory failed to recognise that all human beings are in some ways unique and that they develop their own very individual ways of making sense of the world. According to Kelly, we all have an internal set of mental categories which we use to organise our perceptions. He called these categories personal constructs and developed a technique to discover them - the repertory grid. This technique has been described as follows:[5]

> the subject is asked for the names of ten to fifteen people in certain relationships, eg "a friend of the same sex", "a teacher you liked". The names are written on cards and presented to him three at a time. The subject is asked which two of the three are most similar, and in what way the other one differs, thus eliciting one of his "constructs". When a number of constructs have been found, a "grid" is made up in which all the target persons are rated on all the constructs. Statistical methods can be used to find the general dimensions which are most used by the subject.

Personal construct theory was first developed for use in psychotherapy, for use with individuals. As a result it is not designed to establish broad generalisations about how people perceive one another. However, it has generated a great deal of research and can offer some interesting generalisations:

- men and women seem to use rather different constructs
- some people have very simple construct systems, other people fairly complex ones
- people with very simple construct systems will have a very distorted picture of other people; in extreme cases this can mean that they cannot behave very effectively in social situations

Attribution theory

Attribution theory is a fairly recent development which attempts to explain how people perceive one another. This theory is particularly interested in how people decide the *cause* of other people's actions. It can also be used to examine how we explain our own actions. One way of explaining this theory is to explain the model proposed by Jones and Davis.[6]

Imagine yourself observing another person, A, behaving. You would be able to observe two main things

- A' s **actions**

- the **effect** of A's actions

For example, if A was shouting at X, you could observe this and see what effect this was having on the other person - are they paying attention, laughing, crying or what? Let us assume that X is crying.

Attribution theory now tries to explain what sort of personal impression you gain of A. Do you decide that he is rude, angry, and bullying? Or do you decide that he is doing what he is doing because of the situation he is in rather than because of some aspect of his own character.

According to Jones and Davis, you make a series of judgments about A before you can finally decide on his character. Firstly you decide upon:

- KNOWLEDGE: did A know that his behaviour would have the actual effect, ie make the other person cry?

- ABILITY: was A capable of producing this outcome intentionally? Or did A achieve that outcome by chance? For example, you do not decide that someone is a great golfer on the basis of one lucky shot even if it is a hole-in-one.

On the basis of these decisions you decide upon:

- A's INTENTIONS: what was A trying to achieve?

On the basis of this decision you then decide upon:

- A's DISPOSITION, ie A's personal characteristics.

To return to our example, suppose you decided that A knew that shouting at X would make X cry, and that A is capable of deliberately shouting at someone to make them cry. You would then conclude that A intended to humiliate X and may well decide that A is cruel, nasty or whatever.

If on the other hand you decided that A did not anticipate that his shouting would make X cry, and that A is not normally capable of shouting aggressively at people then you would look for other explanations. You would probably decide that A did not intend to humiliate X but that something else had caused A to shout and X in turn to cry.

This model can be used to explain how different people can arrive at different interpretations of the same incident. Take another mock example - imagine a large family party and focus on three characters - Arnold, an undergraduate student, his Aunt Sally who likes him, and his Aunt Peggy who has always regarded him as a "bit of a tearaway".

The drinks are flowing freely and Arnold is observed drinking rather a lot of punch. Later on in the evening he becomes abusive and aggressive. He calls Auntie Peggy "a silly old cow" and becomes even more colourful in his language to other family members. This upsets quite a few people and Arnold is politely shown the door. How did people interpret Arnold's behaviour? And how can we explain their interpretations, using the attribution theory model?

Arnold's explanation (the morning after)

"I am very sorry. I didn't know the punch was so alcoholic. Normally I'm not able to get drunk so easily. I didn't intend to upset people - it's just not my nature."

Aunt Peggy's version

"He knew exactly what he was doing. He's quite capable of pretending that it's the drink that's doing it. He intended to make a scene as he didn't want to come in the first place. He's a nasty, malicious young tearaway."

Aunt Sally's version

"I'm sure Arnold didn't know he was getting drunk and nasty. He's not capable of doing a thing like that. He didn't intend to make a scene. He'll have to be careful what he drinks next time."

Aunt Peggy clearly sees Arnold's behaviour as evidence for his underlying rather nasty disposition. Both Arnold and Aunt Sally suggest that Arnold's behaviour was caused by the situation - the accidental effect of an over-powerful punch. They do not use the event as evidence of Arnold' s underlying disposition.

Subsequent research has tended to alter some detailed characteristics of Jones and Davis' model but the basic principles remain.

There has been considerable interest in the problem of deciding whether you attribute causes to the person (as Aunt Peggy did) or to the situation (as Aunt Sally did). This seems to depend on a number of characteristics:

Distinctiveness

Is the behaviour distinctive in some way? For example, I have never heard the British disc-jockey Jimmy Saville criticise a record. So when he describes a record as good this does not tell me anything about his own choice - "It's just Jimmy being nice again". If he ever did criticise a record I would see this as very strong evidence of his real opinions. The more distinctive the behaviour the more likely you are to attribute it to the person.

Consensus

If everybody agrees on your impression of X's behaviour then you will be more confident about attributing it to the person.

Consistency over time

If you see X as confident then you will stick to that judgement if your impression does not change with repeated observations.

Consistency over modality

If you see X as generous then you will stick to that judgement if X behaves generously in different situations.

The research has also shown that we are susceptible to a number of biasses which I shall discuss later.

Reconciling the different approaches

As I said earlier the different approaches cannot be simply added together to provide a coherent model of person perception - they are based on rather different assumptions. However, they do point to a number of general conclusions which I can offer about person perception:

Organisation

Our perceptions of other people are **organised.** We do believe that certain characteristics go together in people even if there is no concrete evidence to support these associations.

Perception influences communication

Our perception of other people influences how we communicate with them. Kelley's "cold" students usually did not take part in the class discussion.

Personal bias

Our perception of other people may be more of a reflection of our *own* beliefs about the world than of the other people's behaviour or actual personality.

In an ingenious experiment Dornbusch[7] asked subjects to provide descriptions of other people. He then compared these various descriptions to see how much disagreement/agreement there was. For example, he compared:

- A's description of person C
- A's description of person D
- B's description of person C

As persons C and D were different personalities you would expect A to describe them rather differently. And you would expect A and B to give similar descriptions of C.

In fact the study showed that subjects were viewing different other people by applying much the same constructs - there was typically more in common in A's description of different people, than between A's and B's description of the same person.

Inferences

Our perception of other people may contain quite an elaborate set of inferences and decisions based upon a very wide range of evidence.

This comes out very clearly from analyses of systematic biasses discussed by attribution theorists which I shall examine later.

Resistance to change

Our perception of people may be resistant to change, even in the face of contrary evidence.

We may be "taken in" by a self fulfilling prophecy or we may simply choose to ignore contrary information. There is ample evidence for this in the research on stereotypes which I shall discuss later.

Perceiving the situation

As I said earlier, there has been much less research into the ways we perceive or interpret social situations. However, this is now changing.[8] Thus, there are a few useful points I can make:

Rules
People do recognise the rules which seem to be demanded by a particular situation, even though they may not be able to tell you the rules without a great deal of thought.

Constructs
In the same way that we have a construct system about people, we have constructs about situations. For example, in Forgas' study, students used three major dimensions to judge the social situations they were involved in:

- involvement/non-involvement
- pleasant/unpleasant
- know how to behave/do not know how to be-have

In contrast, the housewives only appeared to be using two dimensions:

- involvement, friendliness/non-involvement, unfriendliness
- self-confidence, regularity/lacking in con-fidence, irregular

People and situations
Our perception of other people is inextricably bound up with our perception of the situation we believe they are in.

How accurate are our perceptions of other people?

There is evidence that some people are much more accurate in their perceptions than others.[9] It also appears that such skill is unrelated to age or experience. You cannot expect to become more accurate in your judgements of others simply by growing older. Unfortunately these generalisations disguise a number of quite complicated issues. For example what does being accurate involve? Suppose you are asked to predict the behaviour of person X in situation A. Suppose you also know that X is an off-duty policeman.

If you happen to know a lot about police training and practices you might have a very good idea that the typical policeman would do behaviour Y even if they were technically off-duty. If X then did Y you would be correct. But you would have displayed your expertise and understanding of police training - you would not really have shown how accurately you can judge an individual's characteristics. There are other problems which crop up in investigating this topic. For example, people's behaviour does change significantly across different situations. What is their "true character"? Does it make sense to talk of someone's "real character"?

It has proved a lot easier to investigate errors or distortions in human perception and there is now considerable research on what those are and how they operate. I shall look at two of these sources of error in more detail - stereotypes and attribution biasses.

Stereotypes

We are all familiar with a number of social stereotypes. A great deal of humour is based upon supposed "facts" about specific social groups: Scotsmen are mean, the Irish are stupid, the Welsh can all sing, etc.

There is, of course, plenty of evidence to refute these categorisations but people may still believe them. And this brings us to a definition of a stereotype:[10]

Stereotypes are generalisations about people based on category membership. They are beliefs that all members of a particular group have the same qualities, which circumscribe the group and differentiate it from other groups.

Not all stereotypes are negative and the targets of stereotypes may agree with the judgement made of them. For example, both the English and the Americans see the Americans as easy-going, casual, informal etc.

Some of the most important implications of stereotyping for the subject of this book are given below. Of course, stereotypes have much broader significance in social life because of their possible influences on an individual's sense of identity, and I shall try to bring out some of these influences by using gender stereotypes in the examples.

Stereotypes as "over-general" beliefs

Surveys of gender stereotypes have found very clear stereotypes associated with the different sexes. For example, in one study of personality traits, men were attributed competency, rationality, and assertiveness, whereas: [11]

traits attributed to women comprised a
warmth-expressiveness cluster.

Researchers also report:

a remarkable degree of cross-national generality in the psychological characteristics associated with men and women.[11]

An interesting illustration of the power of such beliefs comes from that well-known cultural phenomenon - Star Trek. In the pilot proposals for the original television series, producer Gene Rodenberry characterised the "Number One" post as occupied by "a glacierlike, efficient female who serves as Ship's Executive Officer". However, audience tests on the pilot episode ("The Cage") showed that audience reaction to the character "ranged from resentment to disbelief". Rodenberry agreed to drop the character and her personality traits were transplanted onto the alien, Mr Spock, who became Number One. The stereotypes won the day:[12]

> Although Star Trek was a show about the 23rd Century, it was being viewed by a 20th Century audience - who resented the idea of a tough, strong-willed woman (too domineering) as second-in-command.

On a more serious note it is important to remember that the beliefs which underpin stereotypes may be believed by both the target and the groups advocating the stereotype. For example, Brigham reports several studies where women seem to expect to perform more poorly on tasks than men, in ways that reinforce the traditional stereotypes.[11] Happily there is also evidence to show that these patterns may be changing.

Stereotypes as "cues" to action

If you have a strong traditional sex-role stereotype then this will predispose you to act in certain ways. For example, consider the implications of the finding that:[13]

> teachers ... expect higher levels of intelligence, independence and logic from pupils described as possessing typically masculine characteristics.

This expectation will undoubtedly be reflected in some aspects of these teachers' behaviour with consequent effect upon the pupils who have been categorised.

Attribution biasses

Another area of possible bias and distortion in our social perception is the so-called attribution biasses which came to light during the work on attribution theory mentioned earlier in this chapter.

There is not space here to provide a comprehensive survey of these but I can mention a couple of the most "dramatic" to highlight their significance.

Self-serving bias

Earlier in this chapter, I gave examples of errors due to faulty perception. This bias is due to motivaton - ususally the motivation to avoid blame. Forgas notes that teachers often claim responsibility for pupils' success while blaming lack of improvement on the pupils themselves.[14]

"Just world" hypothesis

This is the tendency to believe that people are somehow to blame for any misfortunes that befall them. This is a most unfortunate bias to meet in a judge or magistrate, especially if you happen to be in the dock.

Conclusion

This chapter has tried to highlight some of the major processes underlying our social perception. Almost inevitably the discussion has focussed on "errors" and "distortions" where perception can create misunderstandings and conflict. So perhaps the best way to conclude is by simply summarising major sources of error, using a list adapted from Argyle:[15]

Assuming a person will behave in the same way in other situations

People can behave very differently in different situations, and it is important not to overlook situational causes of observed behaviour.

Trying too hard to construct a consistent picture of the other

Of course, stereotypes can be important here, and there is also the danger of rigid attribution biasses.

Being influenced too much by first impressions

Physical appearance and accent may be especially significant, as may certain corresponding stereotypes.

Making positive evaluations and giving favourable ratings to people from the same background

Being influenced too much by negative points

Making constant errors

This may be the consequence of an over-generalised construct system, whereby everyone is regarded as second rate, aggressive, or whatever.

Lack of attention

This can be a particular problem for people who are too wrapped up in their own dilemnas.

NOTES

1 Experiments like these are discussed in most general introductions to social psychology. A useful discussion which focusses on problems of bias and perceptual distortion can be found in Chapter 2 of:

J. C. Brigham (1986) *Social Psychology*, Little, Brown and Company

2 For a discussion of self-fulfilling prophecies which also relates to this chapter's discussion of attribution theory, see the chapter by J. Richard Eiser in:

H. Tajfel and C. Fraser, eds (1978) *Introducing Social Psychology*, Penguin

3 Forgas' book also provides discussion of the main issues in social perception:

J. P. Forgas (1985) *Interpersonal Behaviour*, Pergamon

4 For an alternative and more detailed summary of the work on social perception and personality traits, see Chapter 6 of:

D. C. Pennington (1986) *Essential Social Psychology*, Edward Arnold

5 One of the most interesting introductions to the repertory grid and the general approach which underpins it is the book by Bannister and Fransella. They also disccuss some of the classic experiments mentioned in this book from a construct perspective - see their chapter 5:

D. Bannister and F. Fransella (1971) *Inquiring Man: The Theory of Personal Constructs*, Penguin

6 For an alternative and more extended discussion of the model by Jones and Davis and other work in attribution theory, see the chapter by Eiser referred to in note 2 above.

7   The experiment by Dornbusch and its implications are
     discussed in more detail on p 79ff of:

     P. Ashworth (1979) *Social Interaction and
     Consciousness*, John Wiley

8   For an overview of the complexities of analysing
     social situations, see the Introduction to:

     A. Furnham and M. Argyle, eds (1981) *The Psychology
     of Social Situations*, Pergamon

9   For a discussion of the accuracy of person perception
     in terms of practical implications, see Chapter 4 of:

     R. Millar, V. Crute and O. Hargie (1992) *Professional
     Interviewing*, Routledge

10   This definition comes from a very detailed analysis of
     the process of stereotyping in Chapter 4 of:

     M. A. Hogg and D. Abrams (1988) *Social Identifications*,
     Routledge

11   See Chapter 10 of the book by Brigham referenced in
     note 2 above.

12   The battles which Gene Rodenberry fought with the
     TV establishment to create the USS Enterprise with its
     integrated crew (including an alien, which was also
     resisted quite strongly!) are described in:

     S. E. Whitfield and G. Rodenberry (1991) *The Making
     of Star Trek*, Titan

13   Possible effects of teacher expectations upon pupils'
     performance are discussed by Colin Rogers in Chap-
     ter 8 of the book by Hargreaves and Colley. He also
     discusses the relevance of self-fulfilling prophecies
     and attribution theory:

     D. J. Hargreaves and A. M Colley, eds (1986)
     The Psychology of Sex Roles, Harper and Row

14   See note 3 above.

15 See Chapter 2.

8

Codes

In this chapter, I shall:

- outline why it is useful to use the concept of codes in analysing human communication
- describe the different codes which are used in human communication
- analyse how these codes work

Why do we need to use the concept of "codes"?

Before I look at the implications of examining human communication as a set of codes, I had better provide a more
detailed definition of a code. Unfortunately different
authors have used this term in slightly different ways. For
example, according to one well-known dictionary of communication studies:

> A code is generally defined as a system into which
> signs are organised, governed by consent...We have
> codes of conduct, ethical, aesthetic and language
> codes.[1]

One of the classic texts on human communication advocates
a stricter definition:

> a code is an agreed transformation, usually one to
> one and reversible, by which messages can be con-
> verted from one set of signs to another. [2]

This text continues to

> distinguish sharply between language which is de-
> veloped organically over long periods of time, and
> codes, which are invented for some purpose and
> follow explicit rules.

An example may make this clearer: The Morse Code. This
code is virtually unchanged since its original invention. It
transforms language into a system of taps and displays the
two important characteristics highlighted in the last quote:

- it was invented for a specific purpose - to allow
  communication using specific technology

- it follows very explicit rules whereby taps of varying length are combined in various ways to

represent letters. Only two types of tap are used - short and long - so as to avoid confusion.

If you know the code then you can communicate with someone else who has the necessary knowledge and equipment. If you do not obey the specific rules then your message will not be understood. However, perhaps the rules are not so specific that there is no room for flexibility or creativity - very experienced users are also able to do things that inexperienced users cannot. For example, a very experienced user of morse code can often identify someone at the other end of the line simply from the way they tap!

Without delving too deeply into the technicalities of different definitions, we can certainly agree that one reason for talking about codes is that any one human language, say English, is composed of a number of different codes depending upon who uses it and how they use it. Specific groups within society can and do develop specific ways of using language which suit their own needs and which may not be readily understood by non-members. Professional jargon is an obvious example. And this is not restricted to the traditional white collar professions! You may have attended a pop or rock concert and overheard the stage crew talking to one another using strange and wonderful terms - bins, eq, monitor, foldback. The crew may be using some words such as bin which do crop up in everyday speech but they have adapted them to have a very different meaning.

One obvious advantage of this special use of language is that it can make communication more economical or efficient. However, problems can occur if the specialist has to communicate to a non-specialist. Unfortunately these problems can sometimes go unrecognised with tragic consequences. For example, there has recently been a great deal of research on the special language codes used by British doctors when communicating with patients. Suppose you experience a stomach pain and consult a doctor. Suppose the doctor asks you "Is your pain chronic?", what do you think this means? Some people interpret a chronic pain as a severe pain, others as a regular pain. Whereas the general use of the term chronic is flexible and variable, the doctor is mentally looking up a specific code book of medical diagnosis. This difference can mean a dramatic difference in how the doctor will interpret symptoms. The doctor is actually asking how regular the pain is, ie is it there all the time or not.

Another anecdote illustrates the potential tragedy which can arise from these sorts of misunderstanding. A patient had received tests for cancer. The doctor told him the tests were negative, ie no symptoms of cancer had shown up. The patient interpreted negative in an everyday sense of the term - bad, not positive, unfortunate etc. He was so worried that he decided he could not face the illness and promptly co-mitted suicide.

Just to make life more complicated, we have many other codes available to us apart from those which are part of language. In the next section I shall discuss what these are and how they interrelate. But a few examples here will illustrate some of the complexities of unravelling human codes.

Many gestures have meanings in one culture which are different or perhaps even the opposite in another. Fernando Poyatos[3] has coined the term "cultural fluency" to describe someone who can not only converse in a foreign language but who can also act and interact in a way which is recognised as appropriate by native speakers of the language. He illustrates some of the potential problems caused by lack of fluency with the anecdote of an American friend visiting him in Madrid. While his speech and language was more than adequate, he caused much consternation at the dinner table by a sequence of very un-Spanish eating habits:

- crisscrossing his fork from one hand to another
- keeping his left hand on his lap
- biting from a bread stick rather than breaking a piece off
- pushing some food with his thumb
- licking his fingers rather than using his napkin

At first sight, this may seem just a trivial example of minor embarrassment. But what if his behaviour had been interpreted as deliberately rude/provocative? And what if the situation had been more important than an informal meal? Specific body signs are associated with specific groups or cultures. There is the reportedly true anecdote of the American spy operating in German-occupied territory in World War II who first aroused suspicion because of a few incidental non-European habits like the way he crossed his legs on sitting down. Crossing legs over at the knee is the standard British/European leg-cross! Whereas putting one foot on top of the opposite knee is a more typical American style. There is evidence in support of this particular cultural variation. How did it arise? Your guess is as good as mine.

But are these examples really good illustrations of messages in code? We do not normallly cross our legs in order to send a message! On the other hand we could do. As we shall see later, one way of gaining acceptance in another culture is to adopt mannerisms which are acceptable in that culture. Even more important is the need to avoid mannerisms which may cause offence. On some occasions in some cultures, crossing your legs would be seen as very rude, ie you would be seen as behaving too casually and informally. Many a foreign explorer may have lived (or not!) to regret certain casual gestures which unfortunately were part of the code of insults or antagonism as far as the local natives were concerned.

What are the different codes we use?

As I have already implied there are a number of ways we can communicate with one another apart from using language. These other codes may not work in quite the way language does, so I do need to specify the different types of code available. Most of the introductory texts in communication make a distinction between verbal and nonverbal codes. Verbal codes are language codes; nonverbal communication (NVC) refers to all those codes which use signals other than the actual words we speak. One typical list of nonverbal codes contains the following:[4]

- Facial expression

- Gaze

- Gestures and other bodily movements

- Bodily posture

- Bodily contact, ie touching other people. This varies dramatically across different cultures. We British use this signal very little except in intimate relationships. We have been described as a non-contact culture!

- Orientation, ie where we sit or stand relative to the other people we are talking to.

- Territorial behaviour, ie how you use the physical space round you. If you imagine organising your office at work, how would you do it in order to make the office more welcoming to visitors? Anthropologists have suggested that we are very sensitive to the space around our bodies and that different cultures use different zones to signify different relationships.[5]

- Clothes and appearance: the meaning of different signals here obviously varies dramatically over time, eg length of hair is an interesting example. Compare the "outrageous" examples of previous years (eg the Beatles and Rolling Stones in 1964) with today's standards and you will see how dramatically those standards and meanings have changed.

- Nonverbal aspects of speech: eg tone of voice, accents, pauses.

This list, although useful and fairly comprehensive, can be criticised:

- it implies that all these signals work in similar ways.

- it fails to distinguish between what some
  authors have called the "dynamic"or changing
  and static features of the interaction. Clothes
  and appearance are normally static unchanging
  features for any given interaction. Gestures and
  facial expression are continuously changing.

- some of the distinctions seem rather arbitrary,
  eg why should gaze be singled out for such special attention?

As a result there have been several suggestions for different
ways of categorising verbal and nonverbal signals. For the
rest of this chapter, I shall use the system proposed by
Fraser.[6] He suggests four communication systems as follows:

Verbal

This is all the words we use, and the ways in which we
organise them.

One of the most interesting features of human language
is the fact that it appears to be unique to us. Although there
have recently been some interesting experiments with mon-
keys and dolphins, no other species seems to have a verbal
system like ours. Consider a few aspects of human language
which we tend to take for granted:

- we can invent completely new words or
  phrases

- we can tell lies

- we can change the meaning of existing words.
  Around ten years ago, the term "gay" simply
  meant "frivolous" or "jolly".

No animal species is able to do all these things with their
communications. And this is largely attributable to the way
in which human language works which I shall discuss later.

Intonation

This includes all those variations in pitch and stress which accompany the words in speech. If we make systematic variations in the emphasis we put on different words then we change the meaning of what we are saying. Imagine the following sentence with emphasis placed on different words in it:

"I don't think you know what you're doing."

Changing the emphasis changes the emotional tone. And this may be especially important in encounters between people from different cultural backgrounds.

Many examples of cross-cultural misunderstanding can be explained by revealing the different speakers' use of different patterns of intonation - different code books .

Consider one simple example[7] - imagine you walk into your local bank and building society with the following simple request:

"I want to deposit some money."

How would you say this sentence? A typical English intonation pattern would be to put some emphasis on "deposit", and to let the word "money" trail off by lowering the voice. This would be accepted by the native English cashier as a friendly polite request.

The same sentence could sound very different when delivered by an Asian who used the English words with a typical Asian pattern of intonation. In this case the speaker would not emphasise "deposit" but would emphasise the phrase "some money" by both a rise and fall during this phrase and saying it more loudly than the rest of the sentence. This could easily be interpreted by the native English cashier as "pushy" or even "rude". Try it yourself by saying the sentence with these two very different patterns of intonation.

The implications of this specific misunderstanding may not be too serious but what if this was the start of a more complex negotiation? There is evidence that this sort of misunderstanding is very common and can be very influential in some important situations such as job interviews.

Paralinguistics

This is all those vocal sounds which accompany speech but which are not the actual words we use.

This includes such phenomena as "ums", "ahs", splutters, giggles, pauses, silence, hesitation etc. Some of these signals seem to have very clear meanings. "Um" is usually a sign of agreement and can be a very useful reinforcer (see Chapter 3). Other signals seem to have much more ambiguous meanings, eg hesitation.

Kinesics

This is all body and facial movements.

Many body and facial movements seem to have a very clear meaning although this meaning can vary from culture to culture. For example one signal that has been extensively studied is eye gaze.

How do these codes work?

We can split this general question down into three more specific questions:

- how does each code operate? ie how is it organised or structured and how does it function?

- what do the codes do in normal conversation?

- how do the different codes relate to one another?

How does each code operate?

The verbal system has understandably received most attention from researchers and theorists and we can analyse the component parts. For example, we can look at the structure of language at various levels, each of which has its own rules and characteristics:

Level of analysis	Definition
Phoneme	Basic unit of sound used in speech

Every human language has a fairly small number of basic sounds (usually around thirty) .These are combined in various ways to create words. Some languages have sounds which do not exist in others, e.g. the Scottish pronunciation of "ch" in loch comes from the Gaelic and does not exist in Standard English.

Morpheme	Smallest meaningful unit of language

This is a word or part of a word. For example, bed contains one morpheme, bedside contains two, and bedridden contains three.

Here we need to look at the meaning of words. And this is where we notice a major difference between human and animal language. For humans, any given word can have different meanings depending on the context in which it is used, eg "give". We also develop our own unique associations for words, eg for me, the mention of raisins always brings back memories of school dinners for reasons too painful to describe.

Utterance	That combination of words which expresses an idea.

Written language is expected to conform to the rules of English grammar, eg every sentence must have a verb. Just to make matters more complicated, spoken language often breaks these rules and yet is perfectly acceptable and understandable.

I could continue this analysis into several more levels but we need to bear in mind some important complications. So far I have used a "bottom-up" analysis of language codes - starting from the smallest units and working up the scale. When we listen to and interpret what other people are saying we also seem to use "top-down" analysis. In other words, because of our tendency to perceive in organised patterns we look for overall structure and interpret the detail in the light of this overall "map".

Another complication is that we can look at language from very different perspectives. For example, Douglas Barnes and Frankie Todd distinguish three main levels of analysis in their discussion of a research project into children's talk:[8]

Level	Characterisation
Form	What is said
Discourse	What is done
Strategy	What is to be accomplished

They use the following sentence as an example to explain the difference between the levels - a boy said to a girl in one of the groups:

"Do you, Diane, think he's a delinquent, Diane?"

At the level of Form, this sentence can be examined using the structural characteristics described on the last couple of pages. At the level of Discourse, this sentence can be described in terms of what it is doing - in speech act terms it is defined as an elicitation, as are most questions. The third level, Strategy, considers aims which may be more subtle or long-term. At this level, the sentence was operating as an attempt to bring the girl into the discussion, as a pressure to participate in the group.

Another complication that is also illustrated by this research is that there is not necessarily a simple or straighforward relationship between the different levels. To use the same example, Diane may react to the question as a straightforward elicitation or in terms of her perception of strategy - what she interprets the boy as trying to achieve. This takes us back to the point introduced in Chapter 2 (p 22f) that our conversation relies upon a complex set of shared assumptions and social knowledge.

This brief discussion of language structures and functions does suggest that we do actually understand a great deal about the verbal system. But there are still very large and embarrassing gaps in our knowledge.

There are even more embarrassing gaps in our knowledge when we come to look at the other systems. At least I can describe the structure of language at various levels. We do not have a corresponding grammar of intonation, paralinguistics or kinesics although some researchers have claimed success in working out these structures.[9] However, most psychologists and linguists would conclude that these systems are still rather poorly understood although we do know what various combinations of signals mean and how they are used. We also know that some codes are more complicated or difficult to interpret than others. For example, children often fail to recognise sarcasm. A sarcastic remark is often distinguished from a sincere remark by the pattern of intonation and it seems that this is quite a complex code to interpret.

What do the codes do?

At first sight this question may seem nonsensical. Obviously, we use the codes to communicate. But WHAT are we communicating? In fact it is useful to analyse three uses for the codes we have described, two of which we introduced in Chapter 2:[10]

Representation

We communicate in particular ways in order to give the other person information, in other words, to pass on our representation of how we see things.

Presentation

We communicate in particular ways in order to present ourselves as the type of persons we are (or would like to be).

I can elaborate this definition of presentation by sub-dividing it into three sub categories and relating them to the following example:

If we are strangers standing at a bus stop and I turn to you and say "nice weather today", I have communicated far more to you than just a simple piece of meteorological information. I may well have communicated some aspects of the following:

Social/personal identity

You will have decided various things about me from my use of words, tone of voice etc. If I wanted to create a particular impression then I could use the different codes accordingly.

Current attitudes and feelings:

You will have probably decided from my tone of voice and posture whether I am feeling happy or sad and whether I really do want to have a conversation or am just being polite.

Social relationships:

I could have established a particular relationship at the bus stop if I had included some form of personal address, ie some version of your name or title. We have already seen how powerful rules of address can be . They are also a very important part of everyday encounter. Consider how you react if a stranger addresses you by your first name, or as Mr X. And are there more subtle rules at work, eg would it make a difference if I said "good morning" or "hello" or "hi!"?

Interaction regulation

When we have a conversation, we are not normally aware of all the signals we use and all the rules we obey in order to regulate the interaction, ie to make the conversation orderly and coherent. In most conversations, people obey a set of simple rules - everybody takes turns to speak, only one person talks at a time etc. If these rules are ignored the conversation breaks down. As the conversation proceeds, the participants have to use specific codes, eg they may use eye gaze to signal when they are ready to speak or when they want to finish speaking. A typical British pattern of signals is given below in the extract from Fraser.[6] This pattern would be very different in other cultures and this can create a very real potential for misunderstanding or conflict, eg when a British person tries to talk to someone from a different cultural background without recognising the different rules in operation.

The conversation may be initiated by mutual eye-contact, indicating that the participants are ready and willing to interact. Once the conversation has started, each person looks at the other intermittently. These looks or glances are directed around the other's eyes, last between 1 and 10 seconds each or between 25 and 75 per cent of each person's total time. The amount of time that each spends gazing at the other is considerably more than that spent in mutual eye contact.

The listener is likely to spend more time looking at the speaker than the speaker at the listener. When the speaker, while in full flow, does look at the listener the latter is likely to nod or give an encouraging vocalization. The speaker, when he starts, probably looks away. When he comes to clear grammatical breaks in what he has to say, the speaker is likely to glance briefly at the listener. When he approaches the end of his contribution he will look longer at the listener. If, however, the speaker hesitates or pauses because he is stuck for a word, or an idea, he is not likely to look at the listener.

How do the different codes relate to one another?

Most of the time, we used the different codes to support and complement one another. For example, a few words of praise can be accompanied by a pat on the back and a smile. However, in many situations the relationship between the codes can be ambiguous or even contradictory. In these cases, the person on the receiving end has to decide what is the "real" meaning.

Why do people send ambiguous messages?

Have you ever talked to someone who is doing something else at the same time. An example could be a boss talking to a subordinate while he (the boss) is checking through his mail. If you were the subordinate and started speaking, how would you feel if the boss did not look at you and gave no signals to convince you that he was listening. You may come to a stop fairly abruptly. And then if the boss said "carry on, I'm listening", what would you do? When I have been in this position, I have sometimes tended to carry on speaking as requested but not put any real effort into it. In other words I believed the non-verbal signals of lack of attention and disinterest and I ignored the verbal reassurance.

One reason why someone (like this hypothetical boss) should behave like he did is that he is unaware of what he is doing. People are not necessarily aware of all the nonverbal signals which they are giving out. This means that you may be giving a misleading impression. Perhaps the boss really was listening!

This also means that it can be difficult to disguise what you really feel. Ekman and Friesen[11] coined the term "leakage" to describe situations where specific nonverbal messages were sent by an individual when he or she was trying to display a different impression. An example was the psychiatric patient who was trying to persuade hospital staff that he was no longer highly anxious. He managed to produce a relaxed facial expression and talk in a confident manner but he gave himself away by sitting in a very tense awkward position.

Are some codes more powerful than others?

The example of the paper-shuffling boss and the concept of leakage both suggest that NVC can be much more important or powerful than the words used in a conversation. One oft-repeated generalisation is that NVC contributes up to 70% of the meaning of an interaction.[12] A less contentious but also common generalisation is that NVC is responsible for the "social meaning" which is expressed in a conversation. In other words, I look to see how you behave towards me in order to decide things such as whether you like or admire me and may ignore what you say.

There is certainly some evidence to suggest that NVC can be very powerful but researchers have begun to question some of the generalisations which came out of the early research. One example of this will provide useful illustrations of the complexity of our nonverbal behaviour.

In the 1970s Michael Argyle and colleagues had suggested that:[13]

> the NV (nonverbal) channel is used for negotiating interpersonal attitudes while the verbal channel is used primarily for conveying information

164

This claim was backed up by the results from a series of experiments where three verbal messages which suggested different attitudes (such as hostile, neutral and friendly) were delivered in each of three nonverbal styles. Subjects were asked to rate the communication they received and it was discovered that the nonverbal message had the most effect. For example, if a friendly verbal message was presented with a hostile nonverbal style then the subject *interpreted* this as a hostile communication.

Ellis and Beattie have criticised these experiments on three counts:[14]

- the verbal and nonverbal styles used could have seemed "exaggerated" and not typical of everyday life

- only one female encoder was used - "an attractive, female student aged 23" - w hich raises the issue of how subjects might have reacted to different encoders

- the subjects were "compelled to attend to the communication" in a way which is perhaps not typical of everyday encounters

When Beattie replicated the experiment using both a male and female encoder, he found a more complex pattern of results. Looking at the hostile-friendly dimension, he found that the typical patterns discovered by Argyle *only* occurred with the female encoder. With the male encoder, the nonverbal component did not outweigh the verbal and this was true for both male and female subjects. Could the "power" of the NVC in the Argyle experiment be attributed to other factors? For example, do we attend more to the NVC of attractive people?

It is quite clear that NVC can have powerful effects. Just how powerful may depend on a range of factors which are not as yet fully understood.

Conclusion

Perhaps the most important conclusion to draw from this chapter is to emphasise the variety and complexity of the codes which human beings use to communicate with one another. As well as having to contend with the general ambiguities which are inherent in such a flexible system as human language, we must also recognise that specific groups in society have developed specialised code books for specific purposes.

The identification of nonverbal codes (NVC) adds further levels of complexity and has particular significance when we examine interactions between people from different cultures or ethnic backgrounds.

We should be cautious in deciding how the different codes operate and how they relate to one another. There is the simple distinction between verbal and nonverbal communication - but this disguises a much more complex set of systems at work which deserve more sophisticated analysis. We still have much to learn about the nature and interaction of the various codes and researchers have begun to question some of the very dramatic and clear-cut propositions which emerged from the early research.

Notes

1　There are several dictionaries of Communication/
Media Studies as well as the one referred to in this
chapter. Comparing their treatment of codes/coding
makes interesting reading.

J. Watson and A. Hill (1984) *A Dictionary of
Communication and Media Studies*, Edward Arnold

2　Colin Cherry produced his influential book in 1957.
An extract which discusses definitions is contained in
the reader by Corner and Hawthorn.

C. Cherry (1957) *On Human Communication*, MIT

J. Corner and J. Hawthorn, eds (1985) *Communication
Studies - An Introductory Reader*, Edward Arnold

3　For an extended (and quite complicated) discussion of
NVC with many references to cross-cultural issues,
see:

F. Poyatos (1983) *New Perspectives in Nonverbal
Communication*, Sage

4　This list comes from Owen Hargie's text on social
skills recommended in Chapter 3.

5　Much of the classic work on our use of personal space
came from the anthropologist E. T. Hall:

E.T. Hall (1959) *The Silent Language*, Doubleday
E.T. Hall (1966) *The Hidden Dimension*, Doubleday

6　See the chapter by Colin Fraser in:

H. Tajfel and C. Fraser, eds (1978) *Introducing Social
Psychology*, Penguin

7　This example is taken from work by John Gumperz
and colleagues who produced the film *Crosstalk* which
was first shown on BBC1 on May 1st 1979. The accom-

panying booklet contains analysis of the examples in the film plus discussion of major issues:

J. Gumperz, T. Jupp, C. Roberts (1979) *Crosstalk*, National Centre for Industrial Language Training

8   Douglas Barnes and Frankie Todd's article on "Talk in Small Learning Groups" is Chapter 4 of a fascinating book which illustrates many of the complexities of studying language:

C. Adelman, ed (1981) *Uttering, Muttering - Collecting, Using and Reporting Talk for Social and Educational Research*, Grant McIntyre

9   This approach was strongly advocated by the influential researcher, Ray Birdwhistell:

R. L. Birdwhistell (1970) *Kinesics and Context*, University of Philadelphia Press

10 See the work of Danziger discussed in Chapter 2 and referenced in Chapter 1.

11 Paul Ekman is one of the major American researchers on NVC. His early work which introduced the concept of leakage appeared in 1969 and he has remained active in research. His more recent texts include:

P. Ekman (1985) *Telling Lies*, Norton

P. Ekman, ed (1982) *Emotion in the Human Face*, Cambridge University Press

12 This statistic derives from detailed experimental work by Mehrabian. How far it can be generalised is open to debate:

A. Mehrabian (1972) *Nonverbal Communication*, Aldine-Atherton

13 The quote comes from the text by Trower et al. See Argyle's 1988 text for a recent summary of his position on the power of NVC.

P. Trower, B. Bryant and M. Argyle (1978) *Social Skills and Mental Health*, Methuen

M. Argyle (1988) *Bodily Communication*, 2nd edition, Methuen

14 See Chapter 9 of:

A. Ellis and G. Beattie (1986) *The Psychology of Language and Communication*, Weidenfeld and Nicholson

Section C

Moving beyond the interpersonal

9

Communication
and groups

In this chapter, I shall:

- outline the most important features which distinguish one-to-one, face -to-face communication from communication in groups
- define a psychological group
- discuss the relationship between group membership and communication
- introduce the particular problems of communicating across group boundaries (intergroup communication)

What makes communication in groups any different from interpersonal communication between two people?

For the moment I shall concentrate upon intragroup communication - communication within one small group. There is considerable evidence to support the view that this is different from interpersonal communication in a number of ways. All of the components of interpersonal communication are relevant, but additional factors need to be taken into account. In other words, in order to understand communication within a group, we need to understand factors which are not relevant when we are only considering two individuals communicating with one another as individuals. For example, think of a group which you participate in. Would you say you were a member of that group? If you do, how important is that membership to you? People do feel and act in certain ways as a result of being members of certain groups. But does it make sense to talk of membership of a pair of people? I would say not, although I am not disputing the fact that pairs of people can have very special relationships, as in marriage.

Social groups do constitute another level of social behaviour which needs to be considered in its own terms. Some early writers took this point of view to rather an extreme position and advocated that there was a "group mind", ie that groups could have consciousness or emotions almost independent of their members.[1] Versions of this view are still prominent in some versions of psychoanalysis. I follow a more moderate line which is summarised in the following quote from Sherif,[2] although you will have to ignore the rather sexist implications and recognise that both men and women can be members of groups!

We cannot do justice to events by extrapolating uncritically from man's feelings, attitudes and behaviour when he is in a state of isolation to his behaviour when acting as a member of a group. Being a member of a group and behaving as a member of a group have psychological consequences. There are consequences even when the other members are not immediately present.

Becoming a psychological group

When does a collection of people become a group? A collection of people is not necessarily a group, in the psychological sense. In psychological groups, the individuals involved recognise that they are members of the group and they are aware of the other members. Membership has some psychological significance. For example, imagine the average bus queue standing waiting for a bus, probably in the rain if British weather is on typical form. Here we have a collection of people. But are they a group? Probably not. They are more likely to see themselves as a collection of individuals who simply happen to be in the same place at the same time. They do not normally exhibit any of the characteristics we usually associate with a psychological group, namely:

Interaction
Members of a group act and react towards one another, and these interactions are liable to develop in particular ways over time so that a regular pattern or structure emerges.

Perception
Members of a group will see the group as "real" and will define themselves as members. They will develop a group boundary, ie a shared definition of who is in the group and who is outside the group.

Norms
I have discussed norms before and I have also commented on the "power" of group norms in everyday life, particularly when we observe very public expressions of group membership such as clothing.

Roles

We have also encountered the concept of role on a number of occasions. At a group level you can think of fairly formal norms associated with certain positions such as chair, or more informal roles which can develop in a group, eg the "joker" who is expected to keep the other members cheerful.

Affective relationships

Group members develop affective or emotional relationships with one another over time. They are unlikely to be neutral or indifferent to one another. And of course relationships between members of a group can be very powerful and long-lasting.

Goals

A group will develop shared goals, purposes or objectives.

You can use these characteristics to describe a two-person relationship but they do not apply in quite the same way. For example, group norms are often agreed and enforced by the majority of members who then police any minority who try to step out of line. The notions of majority and minority do not make sense when there are only two people involved and where we have to look at the individual's use of power.

This set of six characteristics[3] is not the only way to define a psychological group but it does suggest the most basic features. There are a few points to bear in mind though:

Dimensions

It is important to consider each of these characteristics as dimensions which vary along a continuum.

You can represent a group in terms of where it would stand on each of the six dimensions. You can expect any particular group to change in these dimensions over time. For example, different groups will have different degrees of interaction, ranging from groups which only meet occasionally to groups which are in almost permanent contact.

Importance and boundary

This list of characteristics does not suggest which is the most important. This may be different in different situations. For example, a number of studies suggest that as long as people *perceive* themselves as a group then they will act accordingly regardless of how much or little contact they have. The most important characteristic then is the group boundary - the distinction between who is in and out of the group.

Types of groups

There are different types of groups. And different types of group exhibit different characteristics.

But what different types do exist? Tajfel and Fraser offer the following list:[3]

- Family groups
- Friendship groups
- Work groups.

These are easily recognisable in everyday life and they do operate somewhat differently. Tajfel and Fraser also suggest that social scientists have "created" two other types of group with distinctive characteristics:

- Laboratory groups
- Experiential groups

As these two types of group are not immediately recognisable I shall give an explanation:

Laboratory groups

A great deal of social psychological research on groups has involved experiments on groups of students (mainly American) who are brought together for a fairly short period of time. Are they different then to typical everyday groups? Tajfel and Fraser conclude they are very different:

> When we look to see how the defining characteristics of a group operate in this case, we have

problems. Sustained interaction lasts for two hours at the most, and it is only for that period that there is much chance of the members having any perception of group membership. Group goals are minimal, as are internally developed norms. Because the members were selected to be as homogeneous as possible, it is very unlikely that role differences will emerge naturally, and because friends, or enemies, were not permitted to be in the same group affective relations are weak. In fact, laboratory groups are hardly groups at all. More charitably we could argue that many small-group studies are, in fact, controlled studies of only the very earliest phases of group development.

Some critics have even referred to these groups as "nonsense groups" because they have so few of the characteristics we associate with everyday social groups. This criticism is probably over-stated but it does mean we must be *very* careful in applying the results of such studies to real groups. It also raises the broader issue of whether we can generalise from laboratory experimental studies. I would argue that it is possible to make useful generalisations provided you are aware of the limitations of the studies in question.

Experiential groups

In the last thirty years there has been an upsurge of interest in groups which meet in order to understand their own interpersonal processes and develop their members' social skills, ie. their understanding of themselves and others.

To understand the point of experiential groups, you need to understand an important distinction in small group research - the distinction between task and process:

- **task**
  This is what the group does, ie the job or task it is established to carry out.

- **process**
  This is how the group operates, ie how mem-

178

bers relate to one another and influence one another.

For example a work group is likely to have fairly well-defined tasks - the group will have certain jobs to do and there will be sanctions if they do not do these jobs properly. The process of the group includes the various ways in which the members get on with one another. There may be a very cordial atmosphere with a great deal of co-operation or there could be a struggle for leadership with a lot of antagonism. Often these process issues are not discussed openly and any tensions are likely to build up over time until there is an inevitable explosion! For example, one recent text on effective teamwork characterises a number of different process problems which can lead to ineffective groups, such as:[4]

- **battle fatigue**
  This group cannot agree on common goals.
  Meetings are running battles where different
  members try to push their view forward and
  blame others for poor performance to date.
  Morale is low and the real co-operation only
  emerges when a common enemy is identified.

- **father knows best**
  This group has a boss with very clear ideas on
  how the work should be done, who expects
  loyalty and obedience from members and gives
  rewards on that basis. As a result criticism of
  the boss's ideas rarely happens, if at all.
  Creativity may well be stifled - the individual
  who has bright ideas which do not fit in with
  the boss's master plan may well be "shut out".

Whereas in many everyday groups there is an emphasis on completing the task, in experiential groups the main focus is understanding the process as it happens. Of course this process contains a number of different elements, including group members' feelings and reactions to each other, the general atmosphere in the group, and role and leadership issues. As a result of this range of issues, it is not surprising to find many different types of experiential groups with

179

different emphases.[5] For example T-groups aim to develop participants' skills in interpersonal and group processes whereas encounter groups usually concentrate on individuals' self-understanding.

It is very difficult to provide a brief description of experiential groups which can be readily understood by someone who does not have direct personal experience of them. They are very different from most everyday groups but can provide very significant insights into how "normal" groups operate. Unfortunately they have become rather controversial and it is difficult to find a balanced discussion of their virtues and failings. Many general textbooks provide a rather distorted picture. In particular, they emphasise *one* aspect of *one* study which suggests that these groups can harm a significant number of the participants.[6] Unfortunately this study has a number of important weaknesses and limitations and more recent research suggests that the general conclusion is unwarranted. On the other hand there is evidence to suggest that different types of experiential groups benefit different people and that it is important to have an experienced and responsible group leader. Given the appropriate circumstances, these groups can achieve learning which other methods cannot reach![7]

Do groups develop over time?

One fairly common finding is that a small group passes through certain stages of development. These are briefly summarised on the next page.[8]

Stage

What happens to the task	What happens to the process

Forming

The group tries to work out what the task involves.	Members are rather wary and try to test out the atmosphere.

Storming

Members may respond emotionally to the demands of the task. There is dispute over what needs to be done.	There is a lot of conflict and argument between group members and usually a struggle for leadership.

Norming

There is an open exchange of opinions and interpretations and the task is agreed upon.	A friendly atmosphere develops and members take on fairly definite roles.

Performing

Solutions to the task emerge.	People carry out their roles in relation to one another.

This theory of group development appears in most introductory texts in communication. Unfortunately the research evidence does not totally support it. A few alternative positions have emerged.

- other stage theories have been proposed which have some evidence to back them up.[9]

- some researchers have suggested that groups alternate between different phases rather than go through a definite series of stages.
  For example, Bales has shown that some problem-solving groups alternate between a phase where they concentrate on the task and a phase where they concentrate on their personal relationships.[10]

- some studies have suggested that groups do not follow the stages described above in exactly this order. For example there does not always have to be a stage of conflict - storming.

At the moment it is difficult to decide between these alternative models of group development because there is not enough research evidence which looks at natural everyday groups. To summarise the main evidence at the moment, I would say that:

- you can assume that a group is likely to go through certain stages

- the exact nature and sequence of these stages will depend on a number of factors such as the leadership of a group

How does group membership influence communication?

Membership of a group influences communication in a number of ways. Here I only have space to examine two, almost contradictory, influences. On the one hand a group

can develop norms which restrict its members' behaviour
and communication; on the other hand a group can provide
support and understanding for its members and allow them
to express themselves in ways which they otherwise would
not have done.

Conformity pressures in groups

Conformity can be defined as a change in a person's
behaviour or opinions as a result of real or imagined
pressure from a person or group of people.[11]

This definition is fairly typical but does have limitations. It
fails to distinguish between pressures from a group, which
we shall concentrate on in this section, and pressures from
an individual. This latter pressure often gives rise to obedience which is a rather different psychological experience.[12]

The most widely-reported experiment on conformity to
group pressure is the classic study by Solomon Asch which
has been vividly described from the subject's point of view
by Aronson:[13]

Put yourself in the following scene. You have vol-
unteered to participate in an experiment on perceptual judgment. You enter a room with four other
participants. The experimenter shows all of you a
straight line (line X). Simultaneously, he shows you
three other lines for comparison (lines A, B and C).
He asks you to chose which of the three lines is
closest in length to line X. The judgment strikes you
as being a very easy one. It is perfectly clear to you
that line B is the correct answer, and when your turn
comes, you will clearly say that B is the one. But it's
not your turn to respond. The person whose turn it
is looks carefully at the lines and says "Line A". Your
mouth drops open and you look at him quizzically.
"How can he believe it's A when any fool can see
that it's B?" you ask yourself. "He must be either

blind or crazy." Now it's the second person's turn to respond. He also chooses line A. You begin to feel like Alice in Wonderland. "How can it be?" you ask yourself. "Are both of these people blind or crazy?" But then the next person responds, and he also says "Line A." You take another look at those lines. "Maybe I'm the only one who's losing his mind," you mutter inaudibly. Now it's the fourth person's turn, and he also judges the correct line to be line A. You break out in a cold sweat. Finally, it's your turn. "Why, it's line A, of course," you declare. "I knew it all the time."

This dramatic description represents the kind of conflict that Asch's college students went through. Certainly they did become anxious and embarrassed. They did not realise that they were the only subjects and that all the other participants were stooges who had been primed to give the wrong answer on certain trials. But how did the real subjects respond? Was there any incentive for them to "give in" to the group?

It is important to be clear about the pattern of Asch's results. For example, do some people give in all of the time? Or do most people give in some of the time? These two patterns of results lead to very different conclusions on the *power* of group pressure.

Unfortunately, many textbook accounts of Asch give a rather vague description of his results and present an almost overwhelming "victory" for conformity pressure over individual judgement. Asch was certainly surprised by the number of subjects who conformed but it is important to remember two points:

- it is an unusual situation - we expect people to differ in their *opinions* but not in a straightforward and unambiguous judgement. This very unexpected element certainly put extra pressure on the subjects.

184

- most subjects gave in some of the time - only a
  few gave in all of the time

This experiment has been repeated on a number of occasions with similar results. It is usually considered as the classic demonstration of the power of a group to influence its members. This is rather ironic as Asch originally wished to investigate factors which could *decrease* conformity behaviour which he subsequently did with variations on his original experiment.

However, explaining these results is not so easy - we can still argue over why Asch's subjects behaved in the way they did. Why did anyone give in at all given that it was not a decision which had any real consequences for anyone? One factor which is important is that there are at least two different forms of pressure which a group can exert over its members:

- **Normative**
  Members follow the norms of the group because they wish to be accepted and liked by other members. In other words, people wish to be accepted and liked by other members.

- **Informational**
  Members pay attention to other responses as this gives them information which helps to clarify the situation. In other words, people wish to be correct and use other people's responses to help them arrive at the right answer. This may be particularly important in ambiguous or anxious circumstances.

Although Asch's experiment is typically regarded as an example of normative pressure, some subjects clearly felt informational pressures. For example, some suggested afterwards that the stooges responses meant that they must have misinterpreted the experimenter's instructions.

Asch's experiment was taken as the definitive demonstration of conformity pressures for many years. Recently his results have been challenged by two British psychologists,

Perrin and Spencer.[14] They repeated his experiment with undergraduate subjects in a British university and found no conformity at all! They have since repeated the experiment with other groups where you might expect stronger peer pressure and found results broadly similar to Asch's, eg with young unemployed West Indian boys .

They conclude that their experiments show the importance of the broader historical and social context in which investigations are conducted. They suggest that Asch's subjects (American college students in the 1950s) were a generally conformist group because of the time they lived in, ie in the infamous McCarthy period in the US. British undergraduates in the 1980s are a more independent non-conformist group. Asch himself has agreed that these considerations must be taken into account.

Thus, I can conclude that groups do exert pressure on individuals to toe the line in particular ways. How far these pressures will influence individuals depends on a number of factors, including:

- the social context
- the membership of the group
- the group norms
- the nature of the task

So far I have been talking about conformity as it might crop up in typical everyday groups. Given special circumstances, these pressures can be much more powerful.

Irving Janis has coined the term **groupthink** to describe:

a way of thinking in which a cohesive group's need for unanimity overwhelms the members' realistic appraisal of alternative courses of action.[15]

In a very cohesive group, where there is a strong pressure for consensus, groupthink may occur and give rise to mistaken group decisions. Janis was particularly interested in classic blunders made by powerful groups such as the Bay of Pigs invasion of Cuba which was masterminded by a small group of advisers in the US government. No one in the group doubted their decisions although these were obviously suspect to outside observers. Janis proposes several factors necessary for a group to develop groupthink including:

- the presence in the group of powerful individuals who enforce the party line
- strong directive leadership
- strong loyalty to the group
- high pressure or stress
- isolation, where the group members do not have much contact with other individuals

Another example may have been the group surrounding Hitler in World War 2. Thus, Janis does *not* propose that cohesion *must* give rise to inferior decisions, which is an impression sometimes given by textbook accounts. A *range* of factors are necessary before groupthink "takes over". One interesting implication here is that a group can consciously adopt ways of communicating which eliminate the risk of groupthink. Janis has made a number of recommendations along these lines. For example, at each and every meeting, one member of the group is formally given the "devil's advocate" role whose job is to point out potential problems or pitfalls in the groups' decisions.

Another frightening example of group influence concerns the term **deindividuation**. Zimbardo coined this term to describe the situation where individual members of a group "lose" their sense of individuality and fulfil their roles even at the expense of their own moral values. The classic experiment which illustrates the phenomenon was Zimbardo's prison experiment which I described in chapter 6.[16]

The important point about these examples of group influence is that they all depend upon certain patterns and styles of group communication. If the members are aware of these pressures then they can *choose* to communicate in a different way with different end-results. And this brings me to my next section:

Group membership as a liberating influence

Discussions of conformity in groups often portray it as a negative phenomenon which has unfortunate consequences as in the Asch or Zimbardo experiments. However, conformity is a necessary part of social life. Without some acceptance of common standards or values, social life would simply disintegrate. It is also true to say that groups can develop norms which help people to develop more freedom in their actions rather than less. At first sight this may seem a contradiction in terms. A few practical illustrations will help to clarify this:

Therapy groups

In the last thirty years, the work of Carl Rogers has been enormously influential in psychotherapy, the treatment of people who are suffering from some form of mental disturbance. Originally, Rogers worked with individual patients or clients. He developed very pronounced views on how a therapist should behave in a one-to-one situation which included the following recommendations:[17]

unconditional positive regard
The therapist should display warmth and caring for the client (positive regard) and this should not be dependent on the client behaving in a particular way.

acting as a model
The therapist should act in a way which the client can use as an example to copy. The therapist should be perfectly open and honest and be quite prepared to discuss his/her own feelings.

"do not give advice"
The role of the therapist is to help clients work through their own problems and arrive at their own solutions.

One way of interpreting these recommendations is to say that Rogers has provided a specific set of communication rules for therapists. He also hopes that members of the groups will adopt the same rules by following the leader's example.

Rogers started working with groups almost by accident. He soon became very enthusiastic about the advantage of working with groups rather than individuals after he "experienced the potency of the changes in attitudes and behaviour which could be achieved in a group." In practical terms he suggests that groups can have powerful and positive effects by enabling the following chain of events:

- members feel psychologically safe and free to express themselves
- members can express their immediate feelings to one another
- mutual trust develops
- members feel more confident and accepting
- members feel less inhibited and can try out new behaviour
- members can learn from one another

Thus, the norms of the group incorporate trust, acceptance, and innovation. When you feel you can trust others, and that they accept and value your personality then you will not be wary of trying out new behaviour and learning from others. In other words, your communication will become more "open" - you will feel less restricted or embarrassed in discussing personal problems or anxieties. You will develop skills in self-disclosure (see chapter 3).

There is now widespread use of groups in psychotherapy. Although many of these do not follow Rogers' theoretical approach, they usually do claim some if not all of the benefit of group work which Rogers outlined - the development of trust and mutual help. And Rogers' ideas have also been influential in more widespread applications of group-work.

Experiential groups

Rogers felt so strongly about the "liberating" effect of therapeutic group experience that he went on to develop a particular type of experiential group - the basic encounter group. This is designed not as a therapeutic experience but as a way of enabling "normal" people to gain insight into their own behaviour. The role of the leader and the overall process is much the same as described above. Again, Rogers is enthusiastic about the likely outcomes:[18]

> Thus, in such a group the individual comes to know himself and each of the others more completely than is possible in the usual social or working relationships. Hence he relates better to others, both in the group and later in the everyday life situation.

There is evidence to suggest that encounter groups can provide these results although they are perhaps not as "powerful" as Rogers first suggested. What is much less clear is what exactly happens in these groups, and how this creates these effects. Systematic research on these questions has recently emerged but has not yet provided very clear answers. I can conclude though that these groups do develop a structure and atmosphere which enables members to experiment and change. And it is important to stress the role of communication in these groups.

Self-help groups

In the last thirty years, there has been an enormous growth in the numbers and membership of self-help groups and organisations, such as Alcoholics Anonymous, Gamblers Anonymous, SHARE, CARE, etc. Although there is a tremendous variety of such organisations, they do share common characteristics. For example, all these groups attempt to bring about personal change in their members. The obvious example is Alcoholics Anonymous who aim to develop their members' acceptance of their problem and then develop a new life-style to cope with it. Common factors can be identified with other self-help groups which have already surfaced in my discussion of therapy and encounter groups:

- mutual care and support
- sharing of experience
- helping others can also benefit yourself
- common problem or circumstances

Unfortunately there has been relatively little systematic research on these groups. As a result, I can only repeat the point that small groups *can* offer an environment in which people can develop new and innovative behaviour. And the role of communication is crucial. A group can become a vehicle for social support and individual development if it develops the appropriate norms and patterns, eg if members are able to self-disclose and trust each other. Where communication is allowed to develop a dogmatic and authoritarian pattern then the damaging effects of conformity pressures will emerge.

Intergroup communication

Intergroup communication is communication between two or more different social groups which may be small face-to-face groups of the sort I discussed in the last section or more general social groups such as different social classes or ethnic groups. It is important to distinguish between interpersonal, intragroup and intergroup communication. These are different levels of communication and different processes operate at each level.

Examples of intergroup communication would be:

- a negotiation between management and union representatives in a company
- a meeting between two gangs of punks and rockers in a holiday town cafe

As these examples suggest, there can be a a good deal of conflict in intergroup relations and I shall examine this later.

The problem of intergroup cooperation

Most of the research on intergroup relations has examined situations where two groups are in competition or in conflict. In these circumstances, communication is liable to be both important and difficult. There is a fairly consistent set of behaviours which occur in such circumstances and so I shall concentrate on these.[19] They may be observed at two levels:

Within each group

- **Perceptions**
  Members will develop biassed perceptions which they will not necessarily be consciously aware of. They will exaggerate the value of their own efforts and be quite certain that they know the other group's position even when they do not.

- **Group Processes**
  Each group will become very close-knit and conformist. It will concentrate very hard on the task in hand (usually beating the other group!).

- **Leadership**
  Each group will choose leaders who are liable to be authoritarian and hard taskmasters.

Between groups

- **Behaviour**
  Groups will actively discriminate against one another at every available opportunity, and will also seek out opportunities to do so.

The implications for communication are fairly self-evident. Exchanges between the groups are liable to be unfriendly or hostile. Messages will be misinterpreted or misunderstood and there is liable to be a progressive escalation of conflict.

The classic illustration of these phenomena was Muzafer Sherif's summer camp experiments. Sherif was a Turkish professor living in America with an American wife. He became interested in prejudice and discrimination after being the victim of some almost bizarre cases of racial stereotyping. He decided to set up a naturalistic experiment which examined relationships between groups which were in competition to see what conflict might occur and how it might be resolved.

Sherif and his colleagues took over an American summer camp on three separate occasions, in 1949, 1953 and 1954, and dutifully observed and investigated the activities of the participants who were unaware that they were, in fact, experimental subjects. Of the three experiments, the most widely reported is the last one, known as the Robber's Cave Experiment, after the name of the summer camp.[19] The Sherifs were interested in the factors which would create or maintain conflict between the groups. In a recent discussion, Carolyn Sherif described some of the background:[20]

> Our hypothesis was that although the pre-existing differences between groups (religious differences and gender differences and so on) do contribute to the conflict, that for individuals to develop these nasty ways, it was not necessary that they have a long history. To have a realistic confrontation between those groups was a sufficient condition.

There are numerous graphic accounts of the conflict which followed.[21] There were fights (which everyone agreed had been started by the other group); insults were exchanged; the group destroyed each other's property; and, in each and every experiment:

the conflict mushroomed to an almost intolerable level. The staff was extremely hard-pressed in trying to prevent an outbreak of serious disorder

Having created this high level of conflict, the Sherifs took several steps to reduce it:

Social contact

For example, a party was organised so the boys could mix and enjoy themselves with no competitive overtones. In fact, both groups seized upon this opportunity to continue the battle. Cakes and sandwiches make good missiles!

Common enemy

The camp was challenged by another camp at baseball. Boys from both groups were chosen in the camp side. Hostilities were suspended, but only until the match with the other camp was over.

Superordinate goals

This was the only approach that did reduce the conflict. In Carolyn Sherif's own words:[20]

> Our final hypothesis was that the contact between equals, in order to cause change, had to involve interdependence of a kind that required the resources and energies of all the members of both groups. There had to be some goal to be achieved in the environment that they couldn't ignore, but that everyone was needed to do. We called those "superordinate goals".

Why do groups have difficulty in establishing harmonious relationships to one another?

Having established that groups can have great difficulty in communicating with one another on friendly terms, it remains to ask why this should be the case. Must competitions inevitably lead to destructive and unnecessary conflict?

Early attempts to answer these questions suggested that we should look at individual processes. For example, Freud argued that:

> It is always possible to bind together a considerable number of people in love, so long as there are other people left over to receive the manifestations of their aggressiveness.[22]

In other words, hostility to the outgroup is *inevitable* because it works to hold a group together.

Another individualistic explanation was that discrimination against outgroups was initiated by individuals with particular personality characteristics or by individuals who were very frustrated. It had been believed for some time that frustration leads to aggression towards a convenient scapegoat.

These explanations may have some applications but cannot explain many examples of conflict - such as the Sherif experiments where the researchers went out of their way to eliminate any possible individuals who had individual problems.

So researchers turned to explanations which discussed the social groups as groups rather than as collections of individuals. The Sherifs' own explanation can be summarised as the following chain of events:

Realistic conflict of interests
leads to
Competition
leads to
Strong identification with the in-group
leads to
Discrimination against the out-group

A different line of explanation was established by British and European researchers led by Henri Tajfel. Following a series of experiments to test the Sherif's ideas, Tajfel concluded that a more fundamental process of social identification led to the discrimination and conflict. The underlying chain of events was as follows:[23]

Social categorisation
leads to
Social identity
leads to
Social comparison
leads to
Psychological distinctiveness
leads to
Self-esteem

In other words, you place yourself (or are placed) in a particular social category and this becomes part of your social identity. For this to be meaningful, you have to compare your group (category) with other categories. When you make this comparison, you look for something distinctive or positive. Thus, your group is seen as better than the group you have compared yourself with. This satisfies your motivation to be a person of some value, ie you need to have high self-esteem.

The development of this perspective provided inspiration for an upsurge of interest in intergroup problems which is continuing to develop and which has provided useful insights into everyday conflicts and problems.[24]

This book is not the place to offer a detailed comparison of the different approaches. Although the accounts of Sherif and Tajfel are rather different, they are best seen as complementary rather than antagonistic. Both have interesting implications for communication as I explore below. Although Tajfel's theory is broader in scope, it cannot explain all intergroup situations. For example, discrimination between groups does not necessarily follow as a result of relevant social comparison as Tajfel would predict - group membership can mean very different things to different people in different situations, and this needs more investigation.

Furthermore, both Sherif and Tajfel would emphasise that psychological explanation must be seen alongside consideration of social and historical factors. For example, Sherif's summer camp groups were equally powerful. What would have happened if one group had been more powerful than the other? In many real-life situations, we are only too aware that the other group is more or less powerful than we are.

Can communication resolve these intergroup difficulties?

In previous sections we have concentrated on intergroup conflict which is obviously where communication is most important. But can groups communicate with one another so as to avoid unnecessary conflict and discrimination? They can do, but only if they take into account the following points:

- **Awareness**
  Group members should be aware of typical intergroup phenomena so that they can be cautious in their assumptions and opinions regarding the other group. They should not jump to conclusions and develop "us-them" attitudes. In other words, they should try to avoid the typical perceptual biasses.

- **Roles**
  Group representatives should try to avoid win-lose situations and attempt to clarify their group's role and position in any negotiations with the other group.

Communication is obviously very important as it underpins both these points. But it is even more important that the groups actually want to solve any differences they may have. Both the above points depend on members and leaders actually wanting to come to terms with one another, despite their differences. In many situations the differences between groups are so emotionally charged that such willingness will not exist. Without this willingness, it is difficult to imagine strategies which will resolve the conflict.

Alternatively, communication can make matters worse by creating an us-them attitude which is not what the participants really want. A casual remark may be interpreted as condescending and the spiral of discrimination starts!

Conclusions

The factors which are important in interpersonal communication are also important in group communication. During this chapter I have made repeated references to basic concepts and processes from areas such as social identity and social perception. But these notions are not sufficient to explain all aspects of group behaviour. Group membership and group boundaries bring out processes which are not likely in interactions between two people.

This distinction between interpersonal and group interaction cannot be absolute. For example, consider the situation when two individuals meet in roles of group *representatives* . In this situation the important processes are likely to be *intergroup* dynamics. Each individual will act upon their perception of what needs to be done to represent the group, rather than more individual concerns.

Notes

1 The concept of group mind was first popularised by Gustave Le Bon. For a discussion of his work which also discusses the relationship between interpersonal and group behaviour see Chapter 1 in Rupert Brown's book:

G. Le Bon (1986) *The Crowd: a Study of the Popular Mind*, T. Fisher Unwin

R. Brown (1988) *Group Processes*, Basil Blackwell

2 This definition comes from the classic text on group interaction:

M. Sherif and C. W. Sherif (1969) *Social Psychology*, Harper and Row

3 For a more extended discussion of these issues, see:

H. Tajfel and C. Fraser (1978) *Introducing Social Psychology*, Penguin

4 This text contains typical recommendations for effective teamwork:

J. Adair (1986) *Effective Teambuilding*, Pan

5 A balanced discussion of the characteristics of different types of experiential groups can be found in:

A. Blumberg and R. T. Golembiewski (1976) *Learning and Change in Groups*, Penguin

6 The classic study which fuelled the controversy over the potential dangers of experiential groups was carried out by Lieberman and colleagues. Although this study arrived at generally positive conclusions regarding encounter groups, the most quoted chapter is the one which suggests that certain individuals find them very stressful and upsetting. There are also potential weaknesses in the methodology which maketheir conclusions difficult to generalise.

M. A. Lieberman, I. D. Yalom and M. B. Miles (1973) *Encounter Groups: First Facts*, Basic Books

7   For a balanced survey of the impact and effects of experiential groups, see the work of Peter Smith:

P. B. Smith (1980) *Small Groups and Personal Change*, Methuen

8   This theory was first developed by Tuckman in 1965:

B. W. Tuckman (1965) "Developmental Sequences in Small Groups", *Psychological Bulletin* 63, 384-99

9   Alternative approaches to group development are reviewed in:

P. W. Shambaugh (1978) "The Development of the Small Group", *Human Relations* 31, 3, 283-95

K. N. Cissna (1984) "Phases in Group Development: the Negative Evidence", *Small Group Behaviour*, 15, 1, 3-32

10 Bales has been a very influential researcher into social groups and his method of observing group behaviour (Interaction Process Analysis) is probably the most widely used technique. He introduced this technique in his 1950 book and updated it in 1970:

R. F. Bales (1950) *Interaction Process Analysis: a Method for the Study of Small Groups*, University of Chicago Press

R. F. Bales (1970) *Personality and Interpersonal Behaviour*, Holt Rinehart and Winston

11 This definition of conformity comes from:

E. Aronson (1992) *The Social Animal*, 6th edn, Freeman

12 The classic studies of obedience which distinguish it from conformity behaviour were undertaken by Stanley Milgram - the "electric shock" experiments. For a recent discussion of the implications of this work see Chapter 4 in Andrew Colman's book:

A. M. Colman (1987) *Facts, Fallacies and Frauds in Psychology*, Hutchinson

S. Milgram (1974) *Obedience to Authority: an Experimental View*, Harper and Row

13 Solomon Asch summarised his researches in Psychological Monographs in 1956. His earlier book on social psychology also contains very interesting discussions of group influence. Aronson provides a very readable account of the experiments (see note 11 above). For a more recent review of this work in relation to other work on social influence see the book by John Turner:

S. E. Asch (1952) *Social Psychology*, Prentice-Hall

S. E. Asch (1956) "Studies of Independence and Conformity: A Minority of One Against a Unanimous Majority", *Psychological Monographs: General and Applied*, 70, 1-70. Whole No. 416

J. C. Turner (1992) *Social Influence*, Open University Press

14 Perrin and Spencer's reworking of the Asch experiments is described in their 1981 article. Asch responded to their studies in a later edition of the same journal (1981, 20, 223-5):

S. Perrin and C. Spencer (1981) "Independence or Conformity in the Asch Experiment as a Reflection of Cultural and Situational Factors", *British Journal of Social Psychology*, 20, 205-9.

15 See Janis' 1982 book for a detailed discussion of the groupthink phenomenon. For a typical summary, see p 234ff of Johnson and Johnson:

I. Janis (1982) *Groupthink*, Houghton Mifflin

D. W. Johnson and F. P. Johnson (1992) *Joining Together: Group Theory and Group Skills*, 4th edn, Prentice-Hall

16 For a recent overview of research and theory on deindividuation, see p 140ff of:

M. A. Hogg and D. Abrams (1988) *Social Identifications*, Routledge

17 See the disccussion of Rogers' approach in Chapter 7.

18 This quote is from Rogers' book on encounter groups:

C. R. Rogers (1969) *Encounter Groups*, Penguin

19 See Chapter 3 of:

J. C. Turner and H. Giles, eds (1981) *Intergroup Behaviour*, Basil Blackwell

20 See the interview with Muzafer and Carolyn Sherif in:

R. I. Evans (1980) *The Making of Social Psychology: Discussions with Creative Contributors*, Wiley

21 See p 640ff of:

B. H. Raven and J. Z Rubin (1983) *Social Psychology*, 2nd edn, John Wiley

22 For a brief introduction to Freud's approach, see p 36ff of:

G. Gaskell and P. Sealy (1976) *Groups: Course Reader for Block 13 Social Psychology Course 3rd Level* , Open University Press

23 For a recent overview of this work which also relates it to the Sherif experiments and other lines of research, see Chapter 11 of:

M. Argyle (1992) *Cooperation: the Basis of Sociability*, Routledge

24 See the book by Turner and Giles cited in note 19, and Chapter 2 (by Hewstone and Giles) in Gudykunst:

W. B. Gudykunst, ed (1986) *Intergroup Communication*, Edward Arnold

10

Looking back and forward

In this chapter, I shall:

- discuss the issue of mediated communication - how the channel of communication can affect the meaning of communication

- suggest ways in which you can evaluate, further develop and extend the material in this book

How can the channel affect communication?

In Chapter 2, I was rather critical of the linear model of communication. However, it is useful in some respects. It does make it clear that all messages are conveyed through a particular channel of communication. This is not surprising as the two men who first developed the model (Shannon and Weaver) were particularly interested in one channel of communication - the telephone.

So far in this book I have concentrated on situations which involve two people communicating face-to-face. But of course this also involves a number of different channels, eg visual, auditory, kinaesthetic etc. Of course, these channels may not always be fully used even in a face-to-face conversation, and we have already mentioned some of the implications of these different channels. But what happens in situations where communication is mediated by some artificial means, eg by some electronic medium like the telephone?

Different channels may have very different implications, for communication, for example:

- a specific channel will affect the form of information which passes through it

- different channels have different impacts

- different channels have different social meanings attached to them

- particular sorts of messages are more appropriate for specific channels

In a real situation whatever happens will be related to a specific combination of all these implications. They are difficult to separate in practice. A few examples and case studies will illustrate some of the complexities.

The low-fi phone

Modern telephone technology uses some very advanced electronic devices but the actual telephone handset into which you speak is relatively cheap and crude. In each handset there is a small microphone and loudspeaker. Both of these are fairly simple devices which cannot reproduce high-fidelity sound. As a result the tone of voices which you hear is not a very accurate reflection of the tone you would hear if that other person was present. This does not affect us when we are talking to someone we know as we can rely on subconscous processes to supply the "missing" information. But it can lead to misunderstandings when we talk to strangers. You can gain a very inaccurate impression of the other person's personality because of the way their tone of voice has been misshapen by the low-fi of the telephone. Another illustration of a similar effect is the way we can be disappointed when we see radio personalities like disc-jockeys in the flesh. Sometimes, they do not "live up to their voice". This may be partly because they use deliberate effects on radio such as echo machines which add drama and richness to the tone of voice. A historical example would be the number of the stars of the silent cinema who were unable to cope with the demands of the new talking picture. The film "Singin' in the Rain" is a very clever parody of this era, if you need an excuse to watch it for purely academic reasons!

English as it is spoke

Another example is the differences between spoken and written language. We expect written language to obey the rules of grammer and to be reasonably coherent. You may have intuitively felt that spoken language obeys the same rules. It does not. If you want to test the proposition then tape record a conversation and write it down when you play it back. The written transcript will be littered with pauses, ums! and ahs!, repetitions, and ungrammatical phrases and expressions. By the same token, a piece of written English which reads clearly may not be at all clear when read out. You may have suffered from a teacher or lecturer who has written out his notes and simply reads them out. Writing good spoken English is a useful skill which does need thought and attention as any television newsreader or scriptwriter will tell you.

What will happen to the videophone?

A videophone is a telephone which has a television screen attached so that the callers can see one another while they are talking. At first impression, this seems like a very useful idea. Many writers have accepted this at face value without recognising the more subtle implications of different channels of communication. For example, Eyre concludes that it is an "obvious aid to communication".[1]

Unfortunately for the manufacturers of videophones this may not be the case. People use different channels of communication for different purposes, and this applies to the ordinary telephone. People in business typically use the telephone to send short urgent messages. Seeing the other person could actually be a disadvantage here because of the tendency to fill out the conversation with social chat. When you meet somebody face-to-face you do expect to exchange some social greetings but you do not expect to do the same in a telephone call unless you know the person very well. So manufacturers of videophones who have aimed their product at the business market do not appear to have established their product despite quite intensive marketing and advertising. This is obviously affected by economic and technical considerations but perhaps it is also true that manufacturers may have failed to appreciate a basic principle of communication - that the channel of communication does matter to people.

The technology which made the videophone a practical possibility has now been developed in other ways which might have better chances of success. Teleconferencing is the term which has been coined to describe the system whereby people in different parts of the country can conduct a meeting without travelling to meet one another. They are connected up by either a video or audio link. In a video link, the individuals concerned sit in a small television studio and talk to their colleagues in other television studios in other parts of the country. By looking at television sets in the studio, each individual can see all the other individuals involved, usually through a split-screen presentation like the ones used by television quiz shows such as University Challenge.

The main advantage of teleconferencing is the saving in costs which are possible. People do not have to travel great distances with the possibility of overnight stay and hotel costs. But will teleconferencing replace face-to-face meetings? Will people accept that the television channel is equivalent to face-to-face meetings?

Although teleconferencing has been available in this country for ten years or more, it has not made as big an impact as the manufacturers would have liked. As with the videophone, this new channel of communication is not regarded as simply an improved version of older methods. It is different and has its own characteristics. Seeing/meeting someone through television is not the same as a face-to-face encounter.

To illustrate this point I can use a more controversial example of the use of television. There have recently been experiments in the legal system in the USA. Prisoners are not brought to court but stand in front of television cameras in a small studio in the prison. There is a television link to the courtroom as with teleconferenced meetings. The television system has some advantages - it saves transport time and costs and appears to speed up the trials. Many lawyers are unhappy with it though. As one prosecuting counsel put it "When I question someone I want to see what their whole body is doing. I want to see how they're shuffling their feet". And there is quite a lot of psychological evidence that people can disguise their emotions in their facial expressions but may give themselves away in other parts of the body (see the discussion of leakage in Chapter 8).

For these reasons, teleconferencing may not be widely adopted for meetings where there are powerful interpersonal issues involved, eg disciplinary tribunals. But more routine meetings may well be accepted. And people may develop the system to have "new" kinds of meetings. New forms of communication lead to new forms of social gathering: they do not necessarily replace the old forms. In fact the old forms may actually be used more. For example, although cinema attendances have declined dramatically since the advent of television, there are actually more films being watched nowadays. Television could not survive without a regular supply of feature films, which can also attract some of the largest audiences.

Going beyond the story so far

As the main purpose of this chapter is to suggest ways you can develop and expand upon the material in this book, it is not sensible simply to repeat all the major issues and concepts I have used. It is more useful to highlight some basic assumptions which are worth further exploration.

In doing this I shall also highlight potential criticisms of the approach I have adopted. This is an introductory text and so I have had to save space by simplifying some of the arguments. Have I made it look too simple and straightforward?

Interdependence

Having suggested that there are a number of fundamental components to interpersonal communication, I have also emphasised that these components are interdependent. The components interact and depend upon one another. This interaction will depend upon the context and that means we must view global generalisations with some caution (such as the *power* of NVC discussed in Chapter 8).

What I have not explored in any real depth is how these factors interact and how they influence each other. Specific situations may need much more detailed explanations. For example, to return to the discussion of NVC, if NVC is an important aspect of human communication how do we explain situations where it can only play a limited part - such as making a telephone call. How do we actually cope with the absence of all the important visual cues? Derek Rutter has explored this issue in detail and developed a theory of "cuelessness".[2] The basic idea is that we are influenced by the aggregate number of usable cues or signals we can perceive from the other person. We use these cues to form an impression of "psychological distance" - "the feeling that their partner is 'there' or 'not there'" - and this in turn influences the content, style and outcome of the interaction. Using this model you would expect that telephone conversations would create more of an impression of psychological distance and would lead to more impersonal conversations. This is not simply a matter of theoretical interest - it has important everyday implications. For example:

- how do blind people communicate? Do they deal differently with sighted than with other blind people?

- if you know you have to negotiate with another person, do you choose to meet face-to-face or would it be to your advantage to use the telephone?

Social and cultural variables

I have repeatedly argued that social and cultural variables are important. But have I made this point strongly enough? And at what point do interpersonal factors become outweighed by cultural variables? And at what point do economic and historical factors need to be taken into account?

These issues are significant if we try to analyse very complex events from an interpersonal viewpoint. For example, one recent analysis of the Gulf War suggests that a critical factor was the very different use of language codes by George Bush and Saddam Hussein.[3] According to this analysis:

Arabic allows lengthy rhetoric, raw emotion, blatant exaggerations, demands, even threats (not necessarily to be carried out).

This is very far from the quiet and measured style used by George Bush. Does it follow that:

> Arabs (Saddam) watching him on television, saw an unexcitable figure *who couldn't really mean what he said*. Otherwise wouldn't he shout and throw in a couple of fine oaths for good measure?

Assuming that this interpretation of different cultural styles is accurate - and this itself is an issue which requires much more detailed examination - how far can these interpersonal issues influence the outcome of international events?

Skills - behaviour and theory

One implication of my discussion of communication skills is that we *can* change our behaviour and communicate more effectively with other people. I argued that this was not simply a matter of mechanically adopting fixed new behaviour patterns but did crucially depend upon our understanding. Effective communication depends upon our social knowledge and also upon our self-awareness.

One area that has not been emphasised in this discussion is the values or ethical concerns we attach to our communication. For example, I mentioned the topic of assertiveness - behaviour which expresses our needs and wishes in ways which are neither aggressive (trampling on other people's rights) nor submissive (giving up your own legitimate rights). Assertive behaviour is the consequence of adopting a complex set of beliefs and attitudes:[4]

> Assertiveness is about having confidence in yourself, a positive attitude about yourself and towards others, and it is about behaving towards others in a way which is direct and honest.

In Chapter 1, I did say that I was not going to discuss how we *should* communicate. In fact, I have expressed value judgements on examples on several occasions - we cannot fully analyse our communication with other people without invoking ethical or moral judgements at some point. And perhaps this is the point on which to conclude this book. Our communication is the expression of our ideas and values. I hope that I have prompted you to explore your interpersonal communication with a more critical and more sensitive perspective.

Notes

1   See:

E. C. Eyre (1979) *Effective Communication Made Simple*, W. H. Allen

2   For a full discussion of both theoretical and practical implications, see:

D. R. Rutter (1984) *Looking and Seeing*, Wiley

3   This analysis appeared in the editorial column of the magazine *Cross Culture* - 3, 1, Spring 1991.

4   This quote is taken from a recent workbook which provides one of the most accessible and useful introductions to assertiveness training:

A. Townend (1991) *Developing Assertiveness*, Routledge

Index